ORPHAN
Tractors

Bill Vossler

Motorbooks International
Publishers & Wholesalers ®

First published in 1996 by Motorbooks International Publishers & Wholesalers, 729 Prospect Avenue, PO Box 1, Osceola, WI 54020-0001 USA

Motorbooks International books are also available at discounts in bulk quantity for industrial or sales-promotional use. For details write to Special Sales Manager at the Publisher's address

Library of Congress Cataloging-in-Publication Data
  Vossler, Bill.
    p. cm.
  Includes index.
  ISBN 0-7603-0168-9 (pbk.)
  1. Farm tractors—United States—Design and construction—History. 2. Agricultural machinery industry—United States—History. I. Title.
TL233.6.F37V67   1996
629.225—dc20   96-14072

On the front cover: Twin City Tractor was one of the hundreds of tractor companies that didn't make it to modern times. *Andrew Morland*

On the back cover: Top: Samson Tractors were owned by the General Motors Corporation for a time. GMC bought Samson in an effort to duplicate Ford's success. It didn't work out. Bottom: The Common Sense tractor used a single rear drive wheel on a four-plow bottom tractor.

Printed in the United States of America

Contents

Acknowledgments

Many thanks to the people who made this book possible: Todd Strand at the State Historical Society Photo Library in Bismarck, North Dakota; Richard Birklid of Nome, North Dakota, who so kindly offered me his large vault of photos; Danny Roen of Comstock, Minnesota, tractor-identifier extraordinaire; John Wickre of Minneapolis, who researched and gathered information on hundreds of orphan tractor companies; Chad Garner of the State Historical Society of Bismarck; Pat Burke of the St. Cloud Public Library, who was so helpful in getting out interlibrary loan information; John Decker at the Stearns County Heritage Center; Earl Herbranson of Hawley; Lee Klancher, my editor, for his encouragement and help; and to all those who have helped in major or minor ways, and whom I might have bypassed.

And most of all, my long-suffering and persevering wife, Nikki Rajala.

Preface

One day in a small town in Minnesota, a man took a bus from a retirement home on an outing to see old farm tractors. When it was time to leave, the elderly gent wasn't ready to go. "Let me stay!" he begged. "I'll walk back to town with my walker."

This is the effect old farm tractors have on many of us. Ever since I was a child in a farming community in North Dakota, I've loved tractors. I've spent countless hours with C.H. Wendel's *Encyclopedia of American Farm Tractors* and Jack Norbeck's *Encyclopedia of American Steam Traction Engines*, as well as R.B. Gray's *The Agricultural Tractor*. I'm indebted deeply to all three men.

But always, as I read the stories of the size of the back wheels and the stroke and the bore, I wondered about the people. What were their stories? Why did they start these tractor companies? Why did they, or some other force, end the companies, and what were those forces?

Those have been the bits of information I've tried to flesh out in the stories of the companies in *Orphan Tractors*. As much as possible (and it wasn't always possible—history has a way of covering its tracks) that's what I've tried to do: find out about the lives of the tractor makers and their companies.

I hope you enjoy reading about these Orphan Tractors as much as I have researching and writing about them. If you have additional information or corrections, contact me through the publisher and let me know about them.

Bill Vossler

Introduction

All of the tractors in this book are failures. Some are good tractors that failed because of poor business management or insufficient capital, while others are poor tractors doubly doomed with unethical business practices. Whatever the reason, orphan tractors are machines that disappeared.

At one time, there were as many as 180 (and perhaps more) tractor companies in the United States. Only a handful are operating today and only one—John Deere—has survived more or less intact. Orphan tractor companies were most populous from the mid-1910s to the early 1920s, when the infamous tractor wars drove over a hundred tractor companies to an early grave.

Sometime in the 1910s, it became apparent that the tractor was going to do for the farm what the car—particularly the Ford—had done for American society. To meet that perceived need, literally hundreds of tractor manufacturers sprang up overnight.

The companies ranged from true innovators to companies that were no more than an advertisement and hope that enough orders—and cash—would come in to finance the construction of a machine. A large number of the new tractor companies contracted a well-known designer to draw up a tractor for them, and the company then built and sold the machine.

No matter how the company was formed, all were in peril when Henry Ford entered the tractor market in 1917. His new Fordson was small, light, and cheap to build and purchase. The Ford factory could also crank out the Fordson in mass, and would build over 100,000 a year. The Fordson spelled doom for the competitors.

The Fordson drove the other major tractor manufacturers to lower prices and increase the number of features on the tractors. The fly-by-night operators began to dwindle. Beginning late in 1920, with the economy sagging and sales dropping off, Ford and International Harvester began going back and forth with price decreases. In the spring of 1922, Ford dropped the price of his Fordson to $395, which was less than his cost. He intended to drive out the competition and take over the market by storm. International responded by selling its own machines at cut rates—$700 or so—and the rest of the tractor industry was in dire straits. The price battle became known as the tractor wars.

The tractor wars ruined the small companies without the deep pockets of giants like International and Ford, and cut the number of manufacturers from X to Y. Those that survived had to face the Depression in the 1930s, which finished off most of them. This book deals mainly with some of the companies that sprang to life in the 1910s and died off by the 1930s.

There were hundreds of these tractor companies, and this book does not attempt to cover all of them. Instead, a cross-section of those on which information was available are chronicled. Bear in mind that details on most are sketchy, so you won't see the complete history that you would with a company such as John Deere or International, where the company history and the tractors are well-known.

If you have information that is not in this book and would like to see it in print, send to Bill Vossler in care of the publisher.

Chapter One

Avery *to* Custom

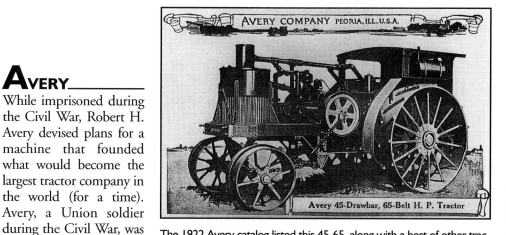

The 1922 Avery catalog listed this 45-65, along with a host of other tractors. To counter the appearance that they made only huge behemoths, their literature also added that boys and girls could easily drive the Avery tractors, and provided pictures of youngsters operating the vehicles to prove it. But by the early 1920s it was too late. Farmers apparently had the impression Avery sold only big tractors, at the same time the farm depression and falling sales began the company's eventual slide into bankruptcy. *Bradley University Collection*

Avery

While imprisoned during the Civil War, Robert H. Avery devised plans for a machine that founded what would become the largest tractor company in the world (for a time). Avery, a Union soldier during the Civil War, was captured and spent time in the infamous Andersonville Confederate prison where inmates routinely died from the abhorrent conditions. What Avery designed in prison was a corn planter, a machine that would plant corn in rows that were evenly spaced to make cultivating more efficient with a higher yield.

After the war ended and Avery was released, he returned home to Galesburg, Illinois, and made a working model of the corn planter by 1869. The planter may or may not have been his first agricultural invention, as the historical records are unclear. In any case, the machines proved to be a successful foundation for Avery. By 1874, Avery was a success.

Avery and his brother, Cyrus M., formed the R. H. and C. M. Avery firm. In 1882, because of better shipping opportunities, they moved to Peoria. In 1891, they began building threshers and steam traction engines, and dominated the market with Avery products for the next 30 years.

The company was renamed the Avery Planter Company. The name changed again to the Avery Manufacturing Company when it bought the Hannah Wagon Company in 1902. By this time, Avery had become a force in American agriculture, with 752 workers and branch offices in Omaha, Des Moines, Kansas City, Indianapolis, Minneapolis, and St. Louis.

When the pair of Avery brothers died in 1905, J. B. Bartholomew took over and renamed the company the Avery Company. At this time, Avery products could be found in the United States and Canada, as well as South America, South Africa, and Russia.

7

This 1915 photo shows an Avery 20-35 two-cylinder tractor at work. The 20-35 was one of Avery's earliest tractors, and its most successful. A number of other variations of the 20-35 came onto the market over the years. This tractor was one of the first ones built by Avery as they entered the competitive gasoline tractor market. Notice the tubular radiator, an Avery trademark on its early tractors. The exhaust, blowing over the top of the radiator, induced a strong draft of air past the radiator, which cooled the water inside. *Richard Birklid Collection*

This about 1910 Avery 20 horsepower was one of the last steamers, used during the heyday of steam threshing. Note the rack at the back of the machine, which allowed the threshers to move quickly from one field to another without hooking up a straw wagon and moving it. Straw was thrown into the burner from the ground. The entire process allowed the threshers to do more work per day. Some farmers actually bought their vehicles for the loudness of the whistles, which would announce to the countryside that this particular engine operator—and as the steam built up in other threshing rigs—that one and that one and that one, were up and ready for work. *State Historical Society of North Dakota*

In 1892, J. B. Bartholomew took over the vice presidency of the company. He was a good man to have around. He invented or improved nearly every device manufactured by the Avery Company. Among the records of the company are three large volumes that contain nothing but letters for patents on farming implements which had been issued to Bartholomew.

One of J.B.'s inventions was the Avery Under-mounted Steam Engine, which was a huge success, and further strengthened Avery's position in the market.

Avery steam traction engines and threshers were the envy of the rest of the agriculture market, although Hart-Parr and other manufacturers slowly began making inroads. To prevent further erosion of their market, Avery in 1909 produced the "farm and city" tractor to be used for small acreages. If they had expanded this line immediately, perhaps their fate would have been different. In 1913, they adjusted their 12-25 to make a nursery tractor.

Unfortunately, they were still stuck on making huge machinery. They constructed a huge single-cylinder tractor of about 65 horsepower. The machine was unsuccessful and was discontinued during the prototype stage. Avery put a 20-35 on the market a year later, and this one worked.

Avery continued to grow, and with it, humane treatment of its workers; Avery established a company dispensary in 1912, employing two doctors five hours a day. They also started an insurance department.

In 1914, they began building gasoline vehicles, first built with wood plug wheels on iron rims. The wood plugs were pounded into wheel holes and formed simple lugs. When the wood plugs wore out, farmers could replace them with new ones.

The year 1916 saw Avery produce a small tractor—the 5-10. The machine was one of the smallest tractors of the time, and it was designed to compete with Henry Ford's soon-to-be-produced lightweight tractor. Avery's oddity had the seat in the middle of the tractor, between the front and back wheels. Despite this miniature tractor and others like it, Avery never put the effort required into small tractors.

In 1917, Avery bought out the Kingman Plow Company land. By this time, more than 2,000 people

An Unbeatable Combination

The Improved Avery Tractor and the Avery Champion "Grain-Saver" Thresher

Avery improved the 20-35 in 1923 from drab black by changing colors—red wheels and gray body—as well as adding fuel tanks under the hood, which was lengthened. This more modern looking tractor also dispensed with the cab, (which totally changed the look of any tractor) and had many other improvements. But it became just another of Avery's many models, and the weight of the many unsold models due to the farm depression caused serious cash flow problems that were never reversed. *State Historical Society of North Dakota*

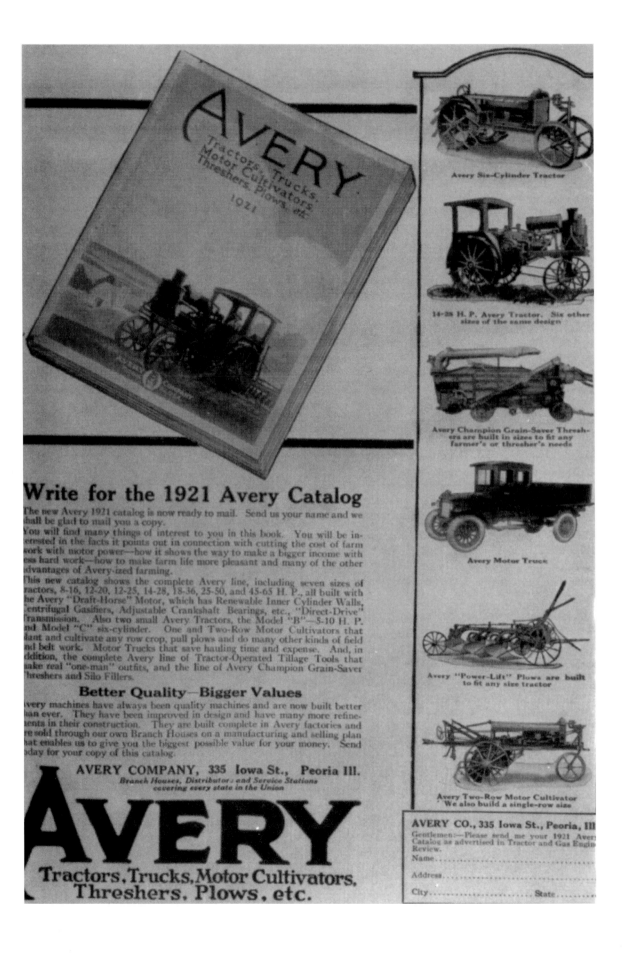

This 30-horsepower Avery was one of the last of the big steamers in the early 1910s and fired with straw. Note the water wagon immediately to the right of the steamers, along with the straw on the rack on the back of the Avery. This picture makes it obvious how labor-intensive threshing was just after the turn of the century. About this time one of Avery's unique methods of gaining new contacts for customers was to offer a free Avery bulldog watch fob in exchange for a list of threshermen, plow operators, or other people likely or interested in purchasing an engine, seperator, or plow. Like many of the Avery steamers, this was an "undermounted" engine, which meant the boiler was on top and the engine underneath. The biggest steamer Avery made was a 40-120. *State Historical Society of North Dakota*

were employed by Avery. They acquired Davis Manufacturing Company , a gasoline motor plant in Milwaukee, so they could build their own gasoline engines. The company continued growing, and everything looked rosy. World War I was on the verge of ending, and along with it the return of men to the farms, of steel production to peace-time uses like tractors, and a new view of farming that required machinery instead of animals.

Left
This 1921 Avery ad details one of Avery's strengths: many choices of tractors, including the 8-16, 12-20, 12-25, 14-28, 18-36, 25-50, and 45-65. All of them were built with the Avery "draft horse" motor, with renewable inner cylinder walls, centrifugal gasifiers, adjustable crankshaft bearings, along with a "direct drive" transmission. The 12-25, 18-36, 25-50, and 45-65 tractors could also be equipped with a special road roller attachment, 32 inches in diameter and 13 1/2 inches wide to help build roads, which every farmer had to do. Three rollers were used for the 12-25, four for the 18-36 and 25-50, and five for the 45-65. Avery also made a motor cultivator and separator, later threshers. Unfortunately, this strength of variety became a liability, because more models meant more inventory, and when the market went bad, Avery was over-extended. *State Historical Society of North Dakota*

In 1920, Avery employed their high-water mark, 2,600 people and produced eight different models of tractors. Unfortunately, many other tractor companies—more than 150 one reference suggests (although it could have been double that number)—existed, and were producing an additional 200 models. Who would have thought that within a year only 10 percent of those 2,600 workers would still be employed at Avery, and less than four years later, the plant itself would go through bankruptcy? It seemed impossible. But it was true.

A severe farm depression struck, and sales of Avery tractors dropped like a stone. The company's earlier strength—a variety of models—became a weakness; when tractors didn't sell, Avery was stuck with costly back loads of parts in inventory for a wide variety of tractors, and that simply pulled them down.

Additionally, they made the mistake many other future orphan tractor companies made at the time—they continued to build heavy tractors, and didn't build enough of the lightweights, which American farmers wanted. To counter their losses from the poor sales of heavy tractors, and additional losses from motor cultiva-

AVERY COMPANY PEORIA, ILL., U.S.A.

An Avery Six-Cylinder Model "C" Tractor
and "Yellow-Baby" Thresher Makes
an Ideal Small Threshing Outfit

The 1922 catalog advertised Avery's new six-cylinder Model C, a small tractor for Avery, compared to the 22,000 pounds for the 40-80 built earlier, the 11,500-pound 20-35, and 7,500-pound 12-25 model. Avery claimed all the problems that could happen to farmers in running other tractors simply couldn't happen with Avery tractors because they had eliminated all the parts on the Avery that caused problems on other tractors. *Bradley University Collection*

Avery 12-Drawbar, 25-Belt H. P. Tractor

This Avery 12-25 was one of the company's attempts to build a small tractor, which was what the average American farmer needed by the early 1920s. The 12-25 also came in a special nursery tractor model, designed by a nurseryman after attending the tractor demonstration in Bloomington, Illinois, in 1915. A special steering device was added, more clearance given, and "coaxers" ran under the entire length of the machine to protect shrubs and branches. *State Historical Society of North Dakota*

This advertisement from the early 1920s exhibits an assortment of Avery products, from the 14-28 tractor operating a silo filler to the Avery track-runner, six-cylinder speed truck, and one-man power-lift "road-razer" for "shaving rough roads and streets smooth." Avery's attempts to satisfy every farm need eventually proved to be their downfall. *State Historical Society of North Dakota*

tors and other products, Avery built a new 15-horse-power tractor with all its gears enclosed and running in oil.

Too little too late. Avery tumbled over the edge, and went bankrupt in 1924. Though records don't exist on how many of the various Averys were made, the numbers were considerable, probably in the top ten of all orphan tractor companies. The Avery Company returned in several different incarnations years later, reorganized in 1925 as Avery Power Machine Company, and made money, but the Great Depression put an end to that. It returned for the final time in 1936 as Avery Farm Machinery Company, making combines, separators, and cylinder teeth, but World War II with its shortage of steel and loss of markets intervened, and added one more company to the death roll.

Just before the merger of the two Bates companies, the Joliet Oil Tractor Company was building the Model D 12-20, as shown in this ad from 1922. The merger was sufficient to keep the Bates Company solvent through the difficult years of the farm depression, from 1920 to 1924, and allowed the company to emerge even stronger, with five different models in 1924. They were one of the first companies, after Holt, to make a crawler. About this time, one man wrote with astonishment that all through the grain belt of the United States, he was seeing the work of two men done with one tractor. *State Historical Society of North Dakota*

BATES

Those who knew Albert J. Bates were not surprised when he invented the Bates tractor. "There are few," says the *Genealogical and Biographical Record of Will County, Illinois*," who possess greater inventive ability than he. This talent was shown even in his early boyhood. When twelve years of age(1875), although he had never seen a scroll saw, he constructed one which was operated by foot power; the steel of a hoop skirt was used for the saw blades by filing teeth in it, and the machine operated successfully. Three years later, long before the days of bicycles in southwestern Missouri, he made of wood a two-wheeled machine with a front wheel of forty-four inches, which did him service for some years; he had never seen a wheel of any kind and was guided in his work solely by the pictures in catalogues."

So it was no surprise that most of the machines used in the Bates Machine Company, and of Bates Tractor Company, were invented by Albert Bates. His history was no more unusual than many children of that day. He attended school in Carthage, Missouri, worked in machine shops as he grew older, worked in a series of factories and shops, and began building machines of his own design. Soon after, in Joliet in 1885, he and his brother organized Bates Brothers, to make wire mill machinery and do general machine work. The demon fire claimed the plant in 1888, and a new one was incorporated as the Bates Machine Company. Bates had many

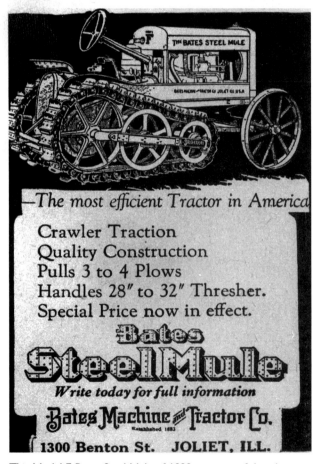

This Model F Bates Steel Mule of 1922 was one of their longest-lasting products, produced from 1921-1937. As times got tough, Bates announced that their model F would be taken "back to pre-war prices" to give farmers a big advantage for spring work. The F used three different four-cylinder engines during its 16 years of production. The fuel tank was hinged at the dashboard to raise it when the engine needed valve work. It was identical to its predecessor (Model D) in all ways except the engine, turning brakes, water air cleaner, carburetor, and hinged fuel tank. Its rating was 18-25 and it weighed 4,850 pounds. *State Historical Society of North Dakota*

business interests that he pursued beyond tractors. He started and owned the Joliet Pure Ice Company , and invented most of its machinery. He essentially owned the Bates-Cotter Company, and he had interest in American Tin Plate Company.

In the early days, his attention was devoted to inventing machinery to make wire fencing. His father, William O. Bates, also worked with him. The Bates machines greatly speeded up the process of making barbed wire and for many years were the standard for the industry. Its products were known and used the world over.

How the Bates Company came to making tractors is unclear, although one can deduce that since they made the Bates-Corliss steam engines, the next logical step was to make a steam traction engine.

Before we get into Bates tractor, there is a point that must be clarified. There were two different Bates producing Bates tractors; the first Bates tractor was the Bates All-Steel Tractor, announced in 1911, and invented by another Bates, Madison F., who may be related. His company, Bates Tractor Company of Lansing, Michigan, was associated with Bates and Edmonds Motor Works, and Olds Engine Works, but had nothing to do with the inventor of the well-known Bates Steel Mule. After 1911, and during the next few years, the Bates (All-Steel) tractor was widely sold, but the Post-War Depression, along with fierce competition among tractor builders, spelled doom for that Bates.

Zoom now to the Joliet Oil Tractor Company. They were selling Bates tractors—different Bates tractors invented by Albert J. Bates. Their 13-30 Bates Steel Mule came out in 1915, and was a more standard-looking tractor than the ones they brought out later; so was the Bates Model H, which was the one with conventional wheel tractors. It was built from 1921 to 1924. The Joliet Oil Tractor Company was building the Bates Steel Mule Model D by 1918. Joliet and Bates Tractor of Lansing, Michigan, then merged in 1919, and became the Bates Machine and Tractor Company of Joliet. The 1919 merger was strong enough to stay in the market through the tough agricultural depression years from 1920 to 1924. By 1924, they were relatively booming, with five different models available. By that time, however, Bates was finding competition in the tractor crawler market less severe, so they put their efforts into crawler tractors, like the Bates Industrial 25, and pulled the Model H off the market. Bates was one of the first companies, after Holt, to make track tractors. A couple of their tracked tractors were curious-looking: The Bates Model F was a strange beast, an 18-25 with regular front tractor wheels, and track-treads in the back.

The Bates Model C was the most memorable design. This was a tricycle layout designed for row-

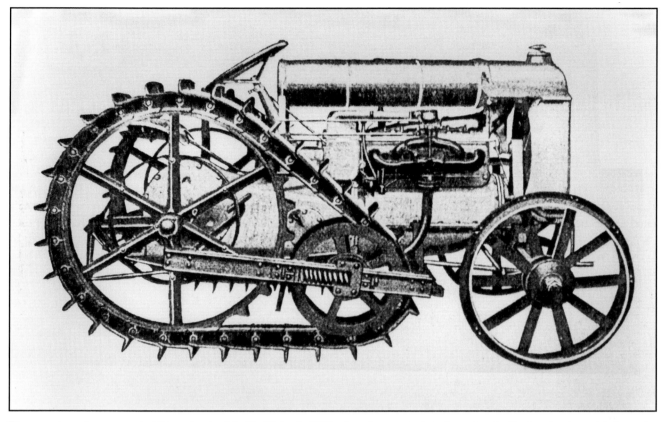

The craze to make one product fit another took hold of Bates in 1922, when they created steel crawlers for Fordson tractors, claiming an increase of 25-60% traction in soft ground. Setup required two hours without drilling holes, making parts, or anything of the sort. The wheels of the tractor had to be taken off, and the crawlers "slipped on." The setup cost $295 in 1922, and was shown at a time when machinery shows at fairs were growing. *State Historical Society of North Dakota*

crop work. At the front two wheels steered the machine, and at the back was a single crawler track, centrally positioned, which transmitted the drive from a chain and track, centrally positioned. It had two widely spaced front steering wheels. It was produced from 1915 to 1918. Their last model, in 1937, was the Bates 40 diesel.

Perhaps Bates survived as long as they did because they had good access to the northern part of the country, which is where most of their machines sold. A University of Chicago Doctor of Philosophy Masters dissertation submitted by William Trout Chambers says, "The chief market territory, however (of Bates Machine and Tractor Co.) is the northern interior of the United States, for proximity to this area and consequent low freight rates to consumers there gives the firm maximum marketing advantages in that territory."

Joliet was an excellent place in which to assemble the materials used in the industry. Most of the metal employed in making machines and machine parts, including pig iron and cast steel used in casting iron and steel parts, and steel plate and structural shapes employed in the fabrication of boilers and making other machine parts, was brought in carload lots from producing plants in Calumet District. Scrap iron of appropriate grades was purchased from dealers in the Chicago District. Most of the coal was brought from mines in the Indiana-Illinois Coal Field, and modeling sand came from Calumet District and other producing areas in Illinois and Indiana. Bates was the only industry in the district that developed steam power to generate electricity.

Joliet was also an excellent location for distribution, as it was located in the Midwest with excellent railway access. Access was augmented by the use of tractors in the construction of highways and roads which went on rapidly in that area since the close of the World War.

In 1929, the year of the stock market collapse, Bates was sold to Foote Brothers Gear and Machine Company. They sold Bates tractors but didn't try to make any new or different ones; the Great Depression was looming.

Six years later, Bates took the plant back; by 1937, the machinery was silent again, and no tractors were being sold. It's unclear how many were made; but it is clear another company joined the list of orphan tractors.

16

This photo of a very early Bull tractor shows a Little Bull from about 1912 sawing wood in the winter at the A.E. Larson farm in Sheldon, North Dakota. Notice the weight ball on the front, a trademark of the early Bull tractors, which possessed a such a light steel front wheel that it needed to be held down to prevent tipping. This was changed to a very heavy cast-iron front wheel, which served the purpose of holding the tractor down. *Richard Birklid Collection*

BULL

It's no bull that the Bull Tractor Company of Minneapolis forever changed the tractor industry in the mid-1910s. Bull created the first lightweight tractor on the market in 1913. At the end of their first year of operation, they had sold more of their Bull tractors (named after its very distinguishing single bull wheel) than any other company in the tractor business. Their sudden surge of sales put other tractor companies out of

Left
In 1917, the Joliet Oil Tractor Company advertised the Bates Steel Mule crawler, the Model C, a 30-horsepower machine that allowed one man to mow 36 acres a day, or harvest 40 acres, or plow 10, or cultivate 31, or drill 50. The company claimed that farmers with regular tractors couldn't get into the fields during the wet springs, unless they had a Bates Steel Mule. It could work on any soil because of its longer pulling surface (where the crawlers met the ground) than normal tractors. The Model C was an odd-looking tricycle-looking machine. *State Historical Society of North Dakota*

business. They operated strictly on cash, which had been unheard of in the tractor business until that time; and they went out of business as fast as they came in.

The Bull Tractor itself might be said to have been, unfortunately, a lot of bull. The price was right, at $335, and sales were over the top. The tractor itself was not a durable product. But when the Little Bull came out in 1913, it was heavily promoted as a tractor destined to change the world, and it was dirt cheap. In those days, when the average buyer was short on mechanical knowledge and even shorter on ready cash, promotion and an affordable price added up to big sales.

In less than a year, Bull was the top producer of tractors in the United States. The three-wheeled Little Bull tractor, much smaller and lighter than most of the behemoths on the market at that time, appealed to them. In addition, the Little Bull clearly pulled deeper and faster than animals pulling plows. It saved time. That was enough for farmers, who flocked to distributors to buy the machine. The company motto was,

These Big Bulls were photographed at a loading dock of unknown location, perhaps at the plant where they were made. This 1915 photo showed the Big Bull, which was, one old-time farmer says, a pretty good motor for their time. A number of them were in use in the Red River Valley of North Dakota and Minnesota at the time. They pulled three plows, but they were so slow they moved hardly as fast as a team of horses walked. When Big Bulls came out, the company and several magazines blamed the downfall of the Little Bull on the farmer's ignorance, saying the machines were used for purposes they were not intended, and the Big Bull was being produced to cover that gap. They were listed at 10-25 horsepower, with a guarantee of 7 1/2-20. *Richard Birklid Collection*

This Little Bull has been restored, and is again in fighting trim. Despite the tractor's shortcomings, it's small size and reasonable price made it quite popular. Who knows what might have become of the company if the Little Bull had been highly successful instead of an abject failure?

"The tractor sensation—does the work of five good horses and sells for the price of two poor ones."

Farmers had been clamoring for smaller tractors for years when D. M. Hartsough and his son Ralph B. Hartsough, who had made tractors before, were asked by P.J. Lyon of Minneapolis to design the Bull tractor. A number of men, all experienced in the tractor business, decided to make some changes in what had become the normal way of doing tractor business—that is, selling lots of iron and not always getting paid for it. They got together and organized Bull Tractor Company of Minneapolis to produce lighter tractors more cheaply so they would more easily see the money when the tractors were sold.

According to Barton Wood Currie, writing in *The Country Gentleman*, "So when they got together in the tractor metropolis of Minneapolis they decided greatly to reduce the tonnage of metal, also to shave down the tonnage of cash, but above all things to get the cash…they have sold their product only for cash and are still selling it for cash only."

P. J. Lyons, who along with Hartsough had run the Gas Traction Company, was the organizer and president, along with J.F. McCarthy of Duluth, Minnesota, and P.H. Knoll, of Minneapolis. Lyons said the price of the Bull tractor was the price of one good horse, and most farmers owned several to half a dozen good horses.

A car dealership in Kansas City switched from selling automobiles to selling strictly Bull tractors because the machines sold for cash only. In 1914, one of the owners of the dealership said the company did $490,000 by October, all of it cash. "We could almost have doubled the business if the factory could have speeded up the output." They said they opened up and closed their accounts simultaneously and required 10 percent down.

The concept of doing cash for tractors was so foreign that a cartoon run in *The Country Gentleman* about the time shows a farmer in a country store holding out a wad of cash, saying, "Well, Henry, I want a new corn planter, a couple of plows, disc harrow, manure spreader, some tools—and here's the cash to pay for 'em!" The store owner was toppling backwards, as were a couple of old salts around the pot-belly stove, while a monkey climbing up the stovepipe also registers shock.

Farm Implements touted the Little Bull in its June 25, 1914, edition: "It is extremely simple—uses only four gears; is three-wheeled (the single front wheel acts as a steering wheel in the furrow); is light and can travel anywhere; very durable." Unfortunately, that last statement was not true. Open gears in the large tractors weren't such a problem because those gears were not down working in the dust; in the Little Bull, the open gears were a problem because dust did their dirty work on them.

The open gears of the Little Bulls allowed dust and dirt to collect and the machines out quickly. The tractor also tipped over easily, and the large number of farmers that bought the machines soon caused an uproar. Bull agents and distributors went to the farmers and offered to give full purchase price against buying the new Big Bull in the hopes of enhancing business. Perhaps it worked for a while, but in 1920, Bull disappeared from the tractor world forever.

Plus, the technology simply wasn't there yet to make small tractors and make them durable. The inventors and builders of Little Bull thought that tractor would simply be a big tractor made small; but the durability of the large tractors did not translate to the smaller one.

Brazenly, the organizers of the company didn't admit that the Little Bull had been a failure. When the Big Bull tractor came out in 1915, *Farm Implements* defended Little Bull as well: "The masses, however, have not been educated to the proper handling of a tractor. For instance, the Little Bull was put on the market as capable of doing the ordinary work of five horses, but too generally it was required to do the work of six or eight horses. It was recommended to pull two 14-inch bottom plows under ordinary conditions, but quite generally it was forced to do this work under extremely difficult conditions, such as plowing in packed soil during a drought, work which no five horses could do. The Big Bull is now put forth to meet these conditions."

Bull agents and distributors went among purchasers of the Little Bull and offered them a bargain exchange by giving full purchase price for the Little Bull in trade on the Big Bull.

Not all of the Little Bulls were reclaimed this way, however. Many of them were working fine in their little niches on the farms where dirt did not greatly affect them, and so farmers wanted to keep them. In other cases, farmers were angered by their experience with the Little Bull and didn't care to try any other Bull Tractor Company products.

Although the Little Bull didn't perform as advertised, it didn't appear that Hartsough was deliberately trying to swindle the customers. A never-ending series of design changes and modifications were adopted in an attempt to cure the problems with the Bull in the field. It was certainly the most modified tractor built up to 1918. Many of these problems may have been eliminated if the tractor had been field tested more thoroughly before being rushed into production. Unfortunately, the modifications almost doubled the Bull's price, putting it

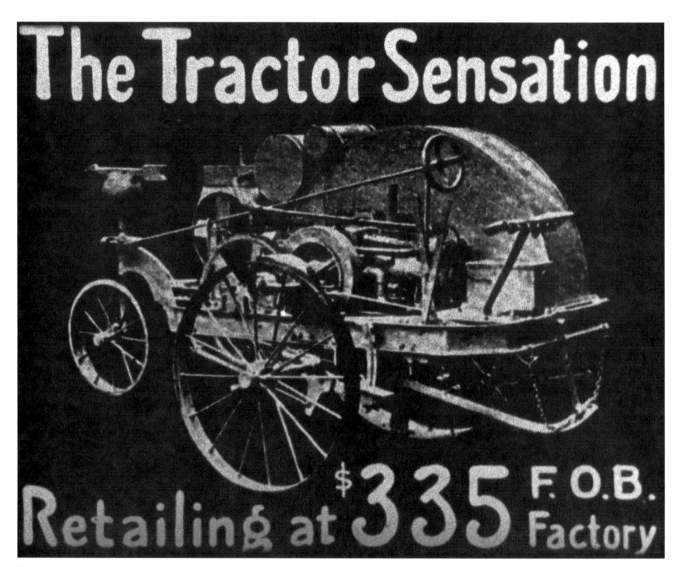

The Little Bull tractor was perhaps the most-hyped tractor ever, and when it came out, it quickly jumped to the top of the best-selling list in 1914. However, after severe mechanical and design problems—it wore out easily because dirt got into its vital components, and it tipped easily—it quickly dropped off the best-seller list, and by 1920, the company went into bankruptcy. Its engine was a two-cylinder, four-cycle, water-cooled type, and it could pull two 14-inch stubble plows in ordinary soil.

within the same price range charged by competitors for slightly larger tractors. Since cost was the major factor in selling tractors in the early 1910s, Bull lost out.

The company woes continued. Hartsough was hired to make another Bull tractor, which he did, but then sold the plans without permission to Lion Tractor Company. Then the company that had contracted to make Bull tractors—Minneapolis Steel and Machine Company—quit making the tractors. After several unsuccessful attempts to get other companies to make Bull tractors, including the Toro Company ("Bull" in Spanish, a company that had been developed to make engines only for Bull tractors), the company merged with Madison Motors Corp. of Anderson, Indiana, to become Bull Tractor-Madison Motors Corp. Tractor Company.

But the damage had already been done. From first place in selling tractors in 1914, Bull slipped to seventh in 1917, and quit making them in 1918. After a 1920 bankruptcy, the company was sold to American Motor Parts Company, and the Bull Tractor Company became an orphan when it filed for bankruptcy.

Measured in terms of its rapid increase in sales and fantastic company growth—nearly 4,000 of the Little Bull tractors were sold in half a year—the Bull tractor was a glorious success. Measured in terms of its mechanical durability, the Bull was a terrible failure.

COD

At first glance, the COD Tractor Company was just another run-of-the-mill tractor company. But at least two things set it apart from other companies. First, that it was formed especially to build Albert O. Espe's latest tractor, and second, the honesty of the company—at least initially.

Albert O. Espe's name is engraved over much of the tractor field, having built his first tractor in 1907, with his designs eventually becoming the Rumely Gas-

This logo for the Bull Tractor Company was used on ads for the tractor, where the advantages of the Big Bull tractor were discussed: that the bull wheel ran in the furrow and didn't pack the land; that the steering wheel ran in line with the wheel and so made the machine self-steering; that it possessed a patented leveling device so the tractor quickly and easily adjusted to side hills or deep furrows; along with electric welded gasoline tanks, and an extra large crank shaft and connecting rod bearings, as well as an extra-large inspection plate on top of the motor, which allowed easy examination of the bearings without disturbing the timing.

This 1915 ad shows the 10-20 COD that was advertised for the Crookston shop, but it is doubtful any were built there, at the $700 price or any other. Notice the tubular radiator, which is similar to the Avery tractors, which were also designed by Albert Espe. This advertisement did what COD seemed to do best, make lists of what they considered the advantages of owning a COD The company claimed one COD tractor would displace 10 horses on the farm.

Pull when Rumely bought out Espe's Universal Tractor, and later designs becoming the Avery tractor.

J.B. Bartholomew at Avery Company paid a great deal for the Espe patents, and put Espe on the Avery payroll. In 1915, the COD Tractor Company was formed in Crookston, Minnesota, to construct Espe's latest tractor design (Espe began building tractors as early as 1907, and was involved in machine shop work for at least a decade before that). In 1916, COD moved to Minneapolis without having built any CODs in Crookston.

The second item that set COD apart was its more straight-forward and honest policy with the farmer. This was a time of turmoil both for farmers and for tractor builders. Hundreds of tractor companies had been formed, and many of them were fly-by-night, and whether intentionally or not, hurt those who invested and lost their money (some people lost their farms), and lowered farmer confidence in tractor companies. Many tractor companies, and their tractors, were not trusted. Farmers had been abused too much, and to make matters worse, they didn't have the mechanical knowledge to fix any of the complicated tractors when they broke down.

That's what COD began to trade upon. In an advertisement, COD Tractor Company tried to convince farmers to switch from horses to machinery. "The tractor is now coming into its own as the solution of difficulties," a COD ad read, "that have so long confronted the farmers of the country. The shortage of men and

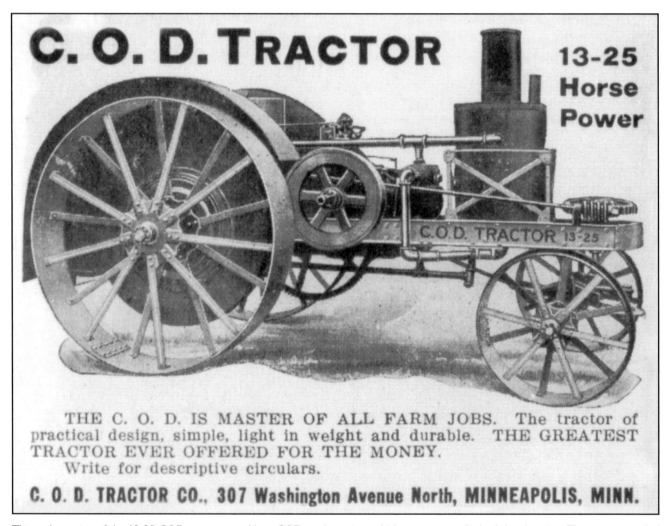

This early version of the 13-25 COD was powered by a COD-made engine, which was a two-cylinder L-head engine. The tractor retailed for $785 in 1915. The COD company was started especially to build this Espe-designed tractor, but the company lasted only four years. St. Paul Foundry & Manufacturing Company ended up selling the tractor, and when the company foundered, had some of the tractors left, which they sold. Others were parted out for a few years afterwards. One North Dakota family invested so heavily in COD that they almost lost their family farm. These were not isolated incidents for people investing in these small tractor companies. Many people were hurt when they went out of existence, not only by having invested in them, but having bought faulty equipment or equipment that could no longer have parts gotten for it or be serviced.

The COD Model B was advertised for the 1918 tractor season, with a few changes from the 13-25 of earlier years, the most obvious being the shape of the radiator and the addition of a fan. It had a special COD steering device, 70x12-inch rear wheels, and 36x8-inch front wheels. It had only two gears, the least of any tractor on the market at the time. In keeping with making it simple, it also had only two levers; one for the transmission, and the second a clutch/brake lever.

This particular COD appears to have been advertised only once, in 1916, but differed from the two 13-25s and the 10-20. No badging is visible, so it is difficult to say what model this is, or even if it was built. Perhaps it is a test model of some sort, a go-between from the 10-20 to the 13-25.

work animals has steadily been increasing for the past few years and has very seriously impeded the successful raising of crops....A good tractor will do the work of six to ten horses and three to five men, and the tasks will be accomplished in less time and more thoroughly and satisfactorily. The cost of the work will also be substantially smaller. And another item that should be considered is the fact that the tractor is no expense to its owner except when it is in operation, while the horses have to be fed when idle just the same as when at work."

Although COD made a laundry-list claim of all the services the tractor could perform on the farm, as indicated in the information from this next advertisement, it seemed to go at the process with more dignity and more honesty than a lot of tractor companies of the time had: the COD would operate the farmer's silo-filler, corn shredder, corn sheller, feed grinder, thresher, and every other belt-driven utility on the farm. Plowing, discing, harrowing seeding, harvesting, road-grading, hauling, and a dozen other similar tasks that were a part of every farmer's job. "...It is a profitable investment for a man farming eighty acres or more."

These last words are astounding, because at the time, tractor companies were essentially telling farmers that a tractor would work for them no matter where they were, no matter the type of soil, the size of farm, as long as they bought "their" tractor. COD Tractor Company seemed more honest.

Another slogan of COD's was, "Make Us Prove It." "We want to prove to you that every statement we make is true. We know what the COD can do and we want you to know it, too. We want you to let us show you by actual inspection and comparison that the COD will do all that we have said, and more."

The tractor industry, during World War I and for a few years after, had numerous problems. Some of these filtered through in an unintentional reading between the lines, as just a few words would tell more about a present problem or fear in the tractor field than will reams of stories. In the case of the COD tractor, it was claimed to be very simple in construction (intimating that other tractors were not simple in construction, and therefore weren't simple to keep up or fix). COD claimed that the troublesome parts had been omitted from this machine (intimating that other tractors still had troublesome parts). And without any intimations, they said that in no other tractor on the market were the parts so few and so simple.

This was a time when farmers—and people in general—did not know a lot about engines and mechanical items, and one of the greatest problems with early tractors was that when things went wrong on

This 1920 shot is of the Common Sense, the first eight-cylinder tractor put into common use. A 20-40, it was rated for pulling four plows, and sold for $2,200. H.W. Adams operated his own tractor school, showing farmers how to operate tractors in general, and the Common Sense in particular. The company got in trouble because of its claim that engineers who passed the Common Sense course could make as much as $15 a day. Common Sense also advertised their tractors to women and children.

them, the farmer, without much mechanical knowledge, often couldn't fix them. So this was supposed to be a tractor that those troublesome things didn't go wrong, and if they did, since it was so simple, it could be fixed.

COD liked to use testimonials in its advertisements. One testimonial to the COD tractor came from a North Dakota farmer: "I will give you my honest opinion of the COD Tractor as I have the opportunity to observe the advantages and disadvantages of a large number of tractors in my work of repairing automobiles and gas engines. I have found that the COD leads them all for an ideal tractor for the average farmer. The COD certainly does all that is claimed for it."

After moving from Crookston, COD tractors were first made in Minneapolis until COD went out of business in 1919. The company left a number of good new machines in the hands of the St. Paul Foundry and Manufacturing Company. Some of those tractors were sold, but others were finally junked or used for parts, which St. Paul Foundry handled for a few years after the demise of COD.

The origin of the name COD is unclear, but was probably named for the three stockholders, Conrad, Ogard, and Daniel. Certainly fewer than a couple hundred of CODs were made, and only five are known to exist. In 1919, the COD Tractor Company disappeared, for reasons that aren't clear, leaving one more orphan tractor sitting in farmers' fields.

COMMON SENSE _____

One day in about 1913, H. W. Adams, who was working for a large tractor concern of the time, was pulled aside by a dealer with whom he was talking tractors. The dealer took him by the arm and led him out around the corner of the store where nobody could hear, and said to him, "Adams, why in the world don't you build a tractor with cut steel gears and enclosed transmission and..." The dealer continued, talking about the exact machine Adams had had in mind for the past couple of years.

H. W. Adams was a different breed of tractor man, and his Common Sense Tractor would be a different breed of tractor, not only because it was the first eight-cylinder tractor on the market, but because Adams took great pains in finding out what the tractor should be like before building it, which included soliciting information from farmers and dealers, and then using it. This was quite different from how most tractor companies—perhaps all—had done their research.

As *Farm Implements* says in its December 31, 1917 issue, "A number of years ago, when a gas tractor that would really work was an object of lively curiosity

This group of rare orphan tractors were photographed about 1920 in front of the buildings at the Fargo Agricultural College in Fargo, North Dakota, after a tractor engineering school class. Good eyes will pick up a Case on the very right of the picture, and a Common Sense in the middle left, and immediately to its left, a Big Bull. The graduates sitting and standing are wearing mortarboards and gowns. Note the cameraman getting ready to take a picture of the graduates and their tractors. The Common Sense school dealt with a variety of tractors, in the hopes that prospective buyers would see the advantages, in comparison, in buying a Common Sense tractor. *Richard Birklid Collection*

to farmers, one of the present well-known manufacturers of tractors was designing and building its first experimental machine. H. W. Adams was at that time employed by this firm and due to his wide experience with steam threshing machines, stationary gas engines, and other power machinery, assisted in designing and building that machine."

The machine was actually shipped to a big farm in North Dakota to be tested to see if it lived up to its expectations. Adams, instead of staying at home and waiting for the farmer to holler, went right along and watched the tractor buck up against actual working conditions. And not just for a couple of passes up and down the field. Adams stayed for two years, working out improvements in design while eliminating the weaknesses of the tractor, until he knew everything he could know. When he returned to the factory, he surprised the officials there with his knowledge and concepts that they hadn't heard anything about.

Adams said, "I knew that too many tractors were the result of theoretical experts who worked on drawing boards, instead of the results given by tractors under actual working conditions in the hands of farmers. I saw where such tractors could not help but fall down, so I decided to start from the other end. I learned first the practical features necessary, and then worked out the proper mechanical methods of obtaining those results. One day I was explaining my ideas to a farmer, and he said, 'well, now you're talking common sense; a tractor like that ought to run.' So I decided to call my tractor the 'Common Sense,' and the name has stuck."

Adams formulated some basic concepts or requirements that his tractor would have to meet. The tractor would have no excess weight to waste power; and an absolute center draft for the number of plows pulled to insure even plowing and lessen strain on the tractor frame; a drive wheel far enough from the furrow to get

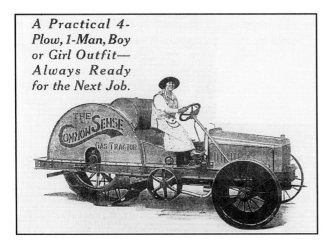

Common Sense was one of the first tractor companies to direct their advertising toward women, as in this 1918 advertisement. The company said it was a practical four-plow, one-man, boy, or girl outfit that was always ready for the next job. Already, information from some of the tractor companies was beginning to be problematic, as this same advertisement says you could get their new free catalog, which was "written in plain English."

solid footing and prevent slippage; all lubricated parts enclosed and running in oil, not sand; perfect accessibility of all working parts, because he knew well from experience that if something goes wrong and the farmer can easily get at it to fix it, he will fix it, but if it is hard to reach, he will let it go, and then his trouble commences; a motor of sufficient power and flexibility to handle all belt work; and a careful selection of the very best material and equipment for every purpose, regardless of cost.

That a company would actually test its product thoroughly out in the field before sending it to market was essentially unheard of in tractor circles at the time, and was the primary reason so many tractors of the time had major problems and ended up bankrupt. Purchasing such a tractor left a bad taste in the mouth of farmers, who were becoming more and more wary. Common Sense took a more rational approach, and didn't want to alienate any of their customers. In fact, quite the opposite: Common Sense asked for farmer input in how the tractor should be made and improved.

In 1915, Adams incorporated Common Sense Gas Tractor Company, in Minneapolis, Minnesota. Common Sense tractors were built very much on the lines of the automobile, which took advantage of mechanical designs that already had been proved to work; again, another practical approach.

The advertising for the 15-25 Common Sense Gas Tractor, in 1915, read, "It has been tried and found true." The rest of the advertising touted the tractor's efficiency, durability, and quality. Of course, in those days, the newest tractors were always compared to the older ones, as in a later Common Sense advertisement for

In this 1918 advertisement for the Common Sense tractor course, the company gives information on how the school has fared, claiming people who took the course were earning two to three times what they had been before they took the course, and that hundreds of people ages 16 to 68 had successfully passed the course. The advertisement stressed that it was not only Common Sense tractors that were worked on in the course, but many different makes of tractors. When Farm Power Sales Company of Minneapolis took over Common Sense a year later, the Common Sense 20-40's specifications were listed as four plows recommended, 400 rpm at normal engine speed, and still two speeds forward, 1 to 3 1/2 miles per hour. Farm Power Sales also began commenting on how the Common Sense was built with the same lines as an automobile.

their "Original eight-cylinder tractor" which said: "Smooth and steady as a steam engine."

A couple of years later, Adams started a tractor school to help educate farmers on how to operate and fix tractors. He focused on Common Sense tractors, of course, hoping the school would net him some sales.

One farmer in Neche, North Dakota, wrote that he decided to pull some huge loads of gravel, 13 or 14 tons each, with his Common Sense tractor. He says 25 people looked on, some having come three or four miles to see him get stuck. They went home disappointed, as the farmer pulled the load with relative ease.

However, trouble was brewing on the horizon. *The Farmer* magazine answered a letter from the Vigilance Bureau of the Minneapolis Advertising Forum in 1917, about claims that Common Sense Tractor Company was making about their Tractor and Auto School. *The Farmer* said the advertisement was more or less exaggerated. One of the claims was that people who went through the school could get paid $5-15 a day. *The Farmer* said they doubted two dozen tractor engineers in the United States were getting $15 a day, and that the six-week class would be enough to help the farmer/trainee learn how to run and fix some of the tractor, but wouldn't make them a master engineer. They said "…We believe the average student gets his money's worth if he applies himself. We think, therefore, you can do a really worth while service to advertisers of this nature if you can show them how they are injuring their own cause by exaggeration…"

That Common Sense would make exaggerated claims was curious, when one considers that Adams knew from the start that the problem with selling tractors was that the claims for what they would do was exaggerated, and he wanted to get away from that, and it seemed so opposite of the stated "common sense" policy of the company.

The head of the Stinson Tractor Company stuck up for Adams, writing that 80 percent of the efficiency depended on the operator, and of course a better-trained operator made for a better-operated tractor, while only 20 percent of its efficiency came from the tractor itself.

Another way the Common Sense Gas Tractor Company was different was that it advertised to women as well as men, showing a picture of a matronly woman in the driver's seat of the eight-cylinder. One farmer said he had his sister operate the machine while he went to lunch, and there were no problems.

However, despite the company's pragmatic approach, something went awry; perhaps lack of funds during the agricultural depression that struck about this time. There is no clear-cut reason discussed anywhere, and Farm Power Sales Company became the successor

to Common Sense in 1919. Little is known about how many were made, and the last mention of the Common Sense Tractor Company was made in an article in 1922, and then the company disappeared into that graveyard reserved only for orphan tractors.

Co-op

In 1934 a number of co-ops—the Farm Bureau Oil Company of Indianapolis, Farmers Union Central Exchange of St. Paul, and the Consumer's Cooperative Association of North Kansas City—decided it was time to market a tractor. But which one? They had a large, ready market and wanted to take advantage of it.

So in 1934 the cooperatives asked Huber Tractor Company of Marion, Ohio, to build a few tractors for them. These were basically the Huber Model L with "Co-op" cast on the radiator and painted red. They carried a Huber serial number. No one knows how many were built, or what model they called it.

Meanwhile, tractor inventor Dent Parrett was also asked to come up with a tractor for Co-op. By late 1934, Parrett Tractors listed a tractor designed by Dent Parrett with a Hercules 1XB four-cylinder engine that had three forward speeds from 1 1/2 to 20 miles per hour.

Parrett's design won out over the lumbering Huber tractors because it represented a more advanced design with the use of the Chrysler engine, standard truck components, pneumatic tires, electrics, and high road speeds.

The first model was unveiled to huge fanfare. According to "The Co-op Tractor: Breaking New Ground," by Robert W. Trevis, on July 22, 1935, "a fire-engine red tractor—unlike any tractor built before—sat in a field near Superior, Wisconsin. Gathered around, nervous and anxious, were Co-op representatives and the tractor's engineers. A man climbed into the tractor seat and pushed the self-starter. The engine caught and ran with a sense of power." The tractor burned gasoline rather than the more common distillate. The Indianapolis Co-op CEOs committed themselves to production and distribution of the Co-op tractor, and thus altered the course of agricultural history.

The three co-ops negotiated a contract with Duplex Printing Press Company of Battle Creek, Michigan, to make the tractors, because Duplex had the heavy equipment to handle manufacturing and assembly; the co-ops would handle sales and distribution. The axles, transmission, and differential were supplied by the Clark Equipment Company.

The first tractor came off the Duplex line in March 1936. Everything looked good. Co-op field men crossed the country with "demonstrator" tractors, and

This Co-op tractor working on a farm in North Dakota shows some of the modern features that made the tractors desirable: headlights, tail-lights, and a cab. In this late 1940s photo, the tractor has a hay-bucker on front and is bucking bundles for threshing oats. With Co-ops built in so many places—Battle Creek, Michigan; Arthurdale, West Virginia; Shelbyville, Indiana; St. Paul, Minnesota—it's hard to figure where this one might have come from, but probably the St. Paul plant. World War II slowed production of Co-ops, but unsold tractors and wholesale defections of the leaders at the plant in Shelbyville after the war put an end to the company.

farmers watched in awe as the rubber-tired tractors easily pulled three 16s (plow bottoms) or four 14s under ordinary conditions, and three 14s in hard pulling.

The cooperatives and Duplex entered into a five-year contract. However, after only two years and 1,775 tractors, Duplex and the co-ops parted ways, because Duplex said the co-ops convinced them to sign a second contract without revealing that the co-ops had entered into another, secret government contract to produce Co-op tractors in Arthurdale, West Virginia.

Duplex said if they had known about the secret negotiations, they wouldn't have altered their first agreement. No more tractors were ever made by Duplex. No one knows how many were made at Arthurdale, or where they were sold.

By 1938 National Cooperatives entered the picture. As the buying organization, it helped set up the Cooperative Manufacturing Company in Battle Creek, Michigan, to continue tractor production and stock

spare parts obtained from Duplex. Co-op Manager C.F. Brown said the greatly improved financial condition of the farmer spurred the decision that a farm cooperative organization would be the logical channel to distribute agricultural machinery, and National Cooperatives could render a real service in this field of endeavor. This huge purchasing power ($60 million) would assure the farmer of lower costs and higher quality. The co-op had over a million members in the United States giving them a ready market.

Farmers Union Central Exchange of St. Paul procured parts to build 150 tractors, which were sold throughout Minnesota, the Dakotas, Montana, and Wisconsin.

Then 15 of National's member regionals soon established the National Farm Machinery Cooperative, and shifted production to a factory in Shelbyville, Indiana, and also purchased the Ohio Cultivator Company at Bellevue, Ohio.

In the winter of 1938–39, Edward Ashley presented a prototype tractor. Two of these prototypes were hand-built in Shelbyville. To get field experience on the tractors, the Co-op did custom plowing and discing around the clock.

They were shown in a field demonstration and at a National Co-op convention. They were then driven back to Indianapolis, serviced, and driven to Mount Vernon, where the Farm Bureau was dedicating their new refinery. On the return trip they were in a July 4th parade in Brazil, Indiana.

Co-op moved into a new factory in Shelbyville, and built a third tractor by hand. It was displayed at the Shelby County Fair and the Indiana State Fair in 1940. Serial number 103 was stamped on the right rail near the brake pedal.

At this point, no more of the Duplex-made tractors were sold in Indiana. Just a few B models were built

This Co-op No. E-4 was built by the Cockshutt Plow Company in Brantford, Ontario, and carries a Cockshutt serial number in series with their production. Cockshutt later called the Co-op tractors they sold, "Blackhawks."

This is a Co-op No. 3 tractor. Co-op probably exemplifies what happens when a committee gets involved with making a product; in the end run, there was nothing wrong with the tractor, but poor management and inefficient manufacture sent it to an early death. One farmer said Co-ops were merely tractors put together out of a wide variety of parts, a Chrysler motor, regular truck rear end, and so on, although he admitted it was a pretty good tractor. Along with Co-op No. 2 tractors, these No. 3s were noted for their high road speeds. Most of them were picked up at the factory by dealers and customers and driven home. They were the only tractors ever driven to the Nebraska tests. Engines on the Co-op No. 3s were six-cylinder Chrysler heavy-duty industrial units with 3 3/8-inch bore, 4 1/2-inch stroke, and 242 cubic inches. Because they went so fast on the roads, they were dangerous, and their rear axle shafts were a bit light to boot. Huber, Parrett, Fate-Root-Heath, and Cockshutt companies all had a hand or a part in Co-op tractors at one point or another.

in 1940; Bs were built in 1941 and 1942, when the war caught up the Shelbyville plant. In June 1942 the factory was converted to military projects. For the last two months workers worked 24 hours a day using up tractor inventory parts.

Other companies were also involved in Co-op tractors: Silver King sold sixty rear-end assemblies that were put in Co-op tractors built in 1939 and called B2 Juniors, the rarest model of all. The front pedestal, hood, and radiator were identical to the B2 model.

Cockshutt of Canada also sold their new tractors with an independent or "live" power take-off marketed under the Co-op name about 1946, called the E series. Some were red underneath and orange on top. Cockshutt also supplied implements to the cooperatives.

By November 1949, 723 Co-op tractors had been sold, but 200 were gathering dust. Of the remaining 200, a Co-op manager wrote, "When these are sold we will not be able to get you any more until after July 1, 1950, because we asked our suppliers to defer shipments of materials and parts for the next run of 500 until July 1, 1950, and they consented. We either sell so many each year, or quit..." Perhaps 4,000 Co-op tractors were sold all together.

The major tractor manufacturers had caught up to the Co-op tractor, and these firms channeled their

sales efforts through implement dealers, not through co-ops which also handled feed, fuel, and fertilizer. No records have been found indicating that any Co-op tractors were built after May 1, 1951.

Custom

It's a long and tortured road to get the history of the Custom Tractor Company, of Shelbyville, Indiana. Even at the end, interpretations differ. Fires destroyed much of the historical record, so part of what remains is hearsay or conjecture.

Edwin O. Ashley, who had been affiliated with making Co-op tractors for a dozen years, decided in early 1945 that he wanted a change. He wanted to build a two-row corn picker. Unfortunately, one of Co-op's affiliates, the Ohio Cultivator Company, made the Blackhawk Corn Picker, and set up a strong front against Ashley, because the Co-op corn picker he proposed would have been directly competing with Ohio Cultivator.

So the heart of the Co-op staff—Ashley, Claude Brown, and Dan Heininger—up and left. They moved about a mile down the road and brought with them dies, plans, blueprints, and their know-how to build Custom tractors.

Heininger never got much credit. He had been the head engineer and head machinist at Co-op. He put everyone else's plans down on paper. Everybody had a lot of ideas, but when it came to manufacturing, Heininger made things work.

Heininger's son, Jerry, of St. Paul, Indiana, says he remembers when Co-op and Custom split. "Dad was troubled by the breakup. In a lot of respects, Brown and my dad had a father-son relationship. Brown was the primary reason dad left."

Everybody was getting war contracts at the time, and within a month after the split, Custom had government contracts. They also had government machines. If you got a war contract, they would set in the machinery for you. You could get almost any machine you wanted in sort of a lend-lease arrangement, which allowed Custom to get going quickly.

The company employed about 70 people at the end of World War II, on three eight-hour shifts. All items manufactured by the firm carried the highest priority rating under U.S. Army Ordnance.

But the company was already looking forward to the end of the war, when they would be making agricultural machinery. The agricultural machinery was already designed and engineered and production was waiting for the green light. During this time Custom even made products for the International Harvester Company.

Custom was a peculiar, low-key tractor operation. Workers recall sitting and working with the head honchos of the company on the assembly line. Whenever work had to be done, anybody could do it. A couple of workers who had never before built anything out of brick and mortar ended up building the painting shed for the factory. The new Custom tractor was essentially a worked-over Co-op Model B with a nearly identical engine, hood stamping, hood design, screens inside, and pedestal. Unfortunately, Custom tractors didn't sell well, and were sent mostly to Canada. The company was sold to Harry Lowther, and when he went bankrupt, the former owners of Custom paid off all the bills to keep the Custom name intact.

Ashley, with input from Brown and Heininger, began working on a new tractor, which was basically a B Model Co-op. The engines, the hood stamping, the hood designs, the screens inside, and the pedestals are all about the same.

They used a regular truck transmission on the early Custom tractors. Later Custom tractors had a stamped steel frame. They went to using a final drive assembly rather than a step-down behind the transmission.

Heininger designed the power take-off for the Custom tractors, as well as the belt pulley. He was also involved in the design of the cultivator system and the hydraulic lift mechanism.

Custom was a peculiar organization. James Badgley of Shelbyville worked at Custom. "I was a welder. Ed Ashley and I used to sit on the front ends of the tractors, and he'd show me where he wanted it welded." None of the 25 workers in the plant knew much so everybody had to shift for themselves. Sometimes Ashley or a foreman would jump right in and give help.

Badgley remembers driving Custom tractors. "Many were shipped to Montgomery Ward in Canada, so we'd take them to the train cars to be loaded. The tractors were all red, except for silver wheels and a few other silver parts. The name was on the front, in white." Badgley road-tested them six miles on the way to storage at Ashley's farm. "They could go fast, so you had to be careful. The row-crop one, you could tip pretty easily," he said.

Heininger says he remembers his uncles getting angry at the tractors. "They didn't like using them for plowing, because they didn't have the pulling power. They used it for discing and cultivating and hay baler type work. But I really enjoyed driving that tractor. It was the fastest thing around at that time, on the road and field."

Ashley was a good person with a quick temper. Ashley did public relations work while Brown was the business end. Workers agreed it was a curious place to work. Workers just did whatever was needed. They started the tractor out, put in the motors, put on the hoods, started the frame on down the line. They scooted dollies from place to place. They even ran parts. The tractor of that day was a simpler machine than today, which meant anyone with a bit of mechanical sense could put the tractors together.

Custom didn't have any implements, which was part of their downfall, because had they had them after the war, when just about anything would sell, they could have established a more solid base. They did make a sort of disc called the Soil Surgeon. It was covered with armored plate that was folded up on the edges, and swiveling knives were attached to the edges of the plate. Custom also manufactured a farm wagon and coaster wagons for kids.

Harry Lowther Company of Shelbyville, and Rockdale, Illinois, had offices in Jacksonville, Florida, Buda, Texas, and Joliet, Illinois, as well. Very little is known about the three models made for a short time by this company, the 96, 97, and 98 Customs. Custom tractors of different types keep popping up, like the Regal Custom, made in Brantford, Ontario.

But eventually, Custom's dreams began to fall apart. The tractors didn't sell well at home in Indiana, and were shipped to Canada.

One might think a lawsuit might have been the company's downfall, since Ashley, Brown, and Heininger brought blueprints and dies when they left Co-op, but evidently the materials belonged to them because there was no suit.

To deepen the mystery, after the two companies separated, Co-op manufactured Custom C models under the Co-op name. A story went around that Co-op wouldn't sue if it was allowed to build some of the C tractors, for which Custom wouldn't sue.

But it was a rapid downhill plunge after only perhaps a couple of hundred tractors were made. Harry Lowther bought the company to huge fanfare, and when it went broke sold it to a Butler, Indiana, company, who sold it to a concern in Hustisford, Wisconsin, in 1952. Hustisford quickly sold it to a Mexican company, where it disappeared.

Later research has discovered a couple of other kinds of Custom tractors: the Regal Custom, made in Brampton, Ontario, with different specifications from the Model B and Model C Customs made in Shelbyville. Also, the Models 96, 97, and 98, made by the Harry A. Lowther Company, a rare tractor known as the Custom fluid drive, and one in California.

Chapter Two

Eagle *to* Gray

EAGLE

Despite stooping to the sensationalized advertising claims of the day, the Eagle Manufacturing Company of Appleton, Wisconsin, built fine machinery and became a major player in gas engines and tractors.

A quirk of nature—a fire—brought one of the company founders to Appleton. Richard Miller's blacksmith building burned down in 1875 in Stephensville, Wisconsin. Miller had a family and needed work, so he moved to Appleton to work with the Appleton Manufacturing Company.

He patented several products, including a swivel hay carrier, and in 1881 formed Eagle Fork Company with partners John Kanouse and William Polifka. Edward Saiberlich

You Can Make Money by Selling
EAGLE TRACTORS
Three Sizes: 13-25; 16-30; 20-40 Model "H"

Powerful medium speed motor, large friction clutch pulley for belt work, driven direct from crankshaft in a position to assure plenty of belt clearance.
A tractor for all needs, SIMPLE, STRONG and DURABLE. Easy to operate and ECONOMICAL.
Pick your size and write for literature and full information.

THE EAGLE MFG. CO., Appleton, Wis.

This Eagle 16-30 was a popular tractor, made for 16 years beginning in 1916, and touted as the simplest tractor built. The Eagle two-cylinder valve-in-head engine was built to be easy to service. Two tractor models were constructed, the F with open bull gears, and the H with shielded bull gears. The Eagle was "the tractor with the troubles left out," the company claimed. Curiously, the Series E Eagle came after the H series, and series G was never made—or never released to the public.

bought out Kanouse and, in 1888, the Eagle Manufacturing Company was incorporated for the purpose of manufacturing, buying, selling, repairing, and dealing in farm implements and hardware.

With these men and others who later joined the company, Eagle was an innovative and curious business concern. The company's initial major product was the stationary gasoline engine, either air- or oil-cooled. In 1905, the company decided to create one of those new-fangled farm machines, the tractor. The company designed and built an opposed two-cylinder engine and installed it in a 12,000-pound tractor. Unfortunately, demand was minimal, few were manufactured, and after 1906, the prototype and engine were not used by Eagle again.

About this time, Eagle proudly advertised that they trusted their engines so much that their 60-horsepower product was used in their own factory to produce power. "We are not doing like some gas engine manufacturers, running by steam because their own product does not suit them to do their work with. Eagle Engines are made for all purposes," they said.

In 1910, Eagle popped back into the tractor market with three sizes, a 16-30, 25-45, and 40-60. During the early 1910s, to meet a demand for a lighter-weight tractor, and probably also as a way of unloading slow-moving stocks of stationary engines, Eagle offered complete traction trucks upon which Eagle engine owners could create their own tractors. These were available for 16-, 22-, 30-, and 45-horsepower units with prices ranging from $425 to $500. Their motto might have been "Make Your Own Tractor!"

In 1911, the *Appleton Post* wrote that a 70-horsepower tractor built in their fair city was making waves. They said that a four-cylinder, 70-horsepower gasoline

Below
In this 1921 ad, Eagle does a take-off of its logo, which usually has a flying eagle just above and to the right of the large E of "Eagle." In this case they substituted the Eagle tractor, as if to say that the tractor was taking off, and perhaps it was, because Eagle was one of the few tractor companies that survived the great agricultural depression of the 1920s.

This Model F 16-30 shown in this ad from 1920 was successful, unlike their first 12,000-pound prototype built in 1906, and scrapped along with the engine almost immediately, and the information gathered put into making better tractors, like this solid piece of equipment. One distinctive feature of the early Eagle tractors was their curious steam-engine sounds, which allowed those nostalgic for bygone steam days to have better equipment but still hear the sounds of the past while out in the fields.

In 1913, Model D tractors were designed to meet the demand for small tractors. The 8-16 and 12-22 used the successful two-cylinder motors with a motor mounted horizontally just ahead of the rear axle. The engine had the crankshafts set at 360 degrees, which gave the distinctive and pleasing steam-engine sounds that many farmers liked. In 1916, the 8-16 sold for $875, the 12-22 for $1,000, and their larger cousin, the 16-30 D, for $1,125.

traction engine was being used by the C. F. Smith Stone Quarry Company to haul stone from the quarry to Appleton. They explained that the engine did the work of at least eight horses, inasmuch as it had a capacity for four wagon loads of stone, 11 cords, with an average of 2,600 pounds to the cord. They said one team of horses could make but two trips per day, whereas the traction engine makes four trips and there is a possibility that this number could be increased with probably one or two more wagons. Its speeds were two to four miles per hour, and the paper noted several times that it did very little damage to the roads.

During the next 28 years, Eagle would make a series of tractors.

Counting the 1906 prototype, the Eagle Company made 20 varieties of tractors, from the two-cylinder opposed, four-cylinder machines, Model D, F, H, and E series, and a six-cylinder series. Curiously enough, Model E tractors came after Model H, and no Model G was built. The letter designations used from 1913 to 1930 have no known rhyme or reason, especially with the

This 40-60 four-cylinder Eagle from 1910 had an engine bore of 8x8 inches, ran at 450 rpm, and weighed 19,000 pounds. It sold for $2,600 in 1915. Rear wheels were huge, six feet in diameter, and the belt pulley was two feet in diameter and a foot wide. The 40-60 came at a good time for Eagle, getting the moribund company going again after a slow time in the 1910s. They were probably produced until 1916.

Model E designation being slipped in after the Model H.

One of the great attractions of the Eagle tractors, besides their durability and usefulness, was the distinctive sound the gasoline motors made, which was much like that of a steam engine. The sound of the Eagle tractors was likely a conscious decision, like Will Durant's decision to put reins on the Samson "Iron Horse" tractor. With the Eagle, farmers could work out in the fields and have the sense they were still piloting the big old steamers, which many loved.

But not everything went well with the company. Eagle was nailed for questionable advertising by the people who ran the Nebraska tests. In the concluding remarks, the testers were concerned that certain company claims in their advertising literature were not necessarily borne out on in the tests. These included the effectiveness of the air breather, quality of engine governing, and claims that the engine ran as well on kerosene as on gasoline.

Like almost every orphan tractor company, Eagle made a wide variety of other products: engine/saw combinations, feed cutters, cutter-blowers, elevators, sweep type horsepowers, power jacks, saw rigs, burring mills, grain grinders, fodder and ensilage cutters, silo fillers, iron and woodworking machinery, farm implements of all types, perhaps even hay presses. Information on how many Eagles were made is unclear.

Eagle also had a branch office in Mankato, Minnesota, to sell to the west; Waterloo Manufacturing Company of Waterloo, Ontario, resold and rebuilt Eagles as well.

In the late 1930s, Eagle hit another snag: they hired a design expert who had worked at Allis-Chalmers, and their newest tractor, the Eagle 6B, showed a front end design strikingly similar to the contemporary Allis-Chalmers Model WC tractors. The front grille, frame, and pedestal were quite similar. AC threatened legal action.

In the end run, it was the economy and failure to innovate that did Eagle in; the Great Depression saw stockholders receive no dividends, and in 1941, they determined to unload the company, receiving 10 cents to the dollar on their stocks when they sold it to Four

The 20-40 Eagle special was a heavily-built tractor and led to the 22-45, with its larger engine block. Some of the Eagle tractors had problems with the governor, and the Model H series had crankshaft problems. The company weathered these minor crises and lasted until the early 1940s.

Wheel Drive Auto Company of Clintonville, Wisconsin. Eagle failed to recognize a need to change with the times, and it learned too late that its products had been eclipsed by more modern versions.

Another fine tractor bit the dust.

FLOUR CITY

When Owen B. Kinnard was asked by a newspaper reporter, "Who made the first tractor? You or Charlie Parr?" Kinnard answered, "Neither one of us. Some Philadelphia mechanic really deserves the credit. But he never got onto the market with his story, so Charlie Hart and Charlie Parr and I claimed the glory."

Kinnard moved from Indiana to Minneapolis in 1881, and began Kinnard and Haines with Albert Haines in 1882. The Minneapolis city directory of the time lists them as machinists.

In 1889, the name was changed to Kinnard Press Company, and in conjunction with a contract with John Deere, they made John Deere hay presses and powers, and the other machinery that had been made by John Deere. Shortly thereafter they also built a larger plant because the demand for farm implements had skyrocketed.

In 1896, the company began work on a gasoline engine of their own design and pattern. There is some confusion as to when it first came out. A history of the company says the machine was to have been on the market by the following spring, but there is no evidence that any were available for purchase before August 1898, when "Flour City" portable and stationary engines were first advertised.

A number of secondary sources have stated that the company first built a gasoline tractor in 1897. No contemporary accounts have been found to corroborate this statement. Trade magazines and advertisements mentioned the gas engines in 1898 and 1899, but never a traction engine until August 1899, when it was noted that the Kinnard Press Company had designed a gasoline traction engine which they did not plan to introduce until 1900, when a considerable number were to be made.

Farm Implements said in its Nov. 23, 1899, issue that a gasoline traction engine would be made by Kinnard in the next year, with the first one ready for operation just after January first. The machines would be giv-

This 1914 photo shows a Flour City 30-50 plowing sod in North Dakota with a six-bottom plow. The back wheels are seven feet tall on this large Flour City tractor. The design for 20-, 30-, and 40-horsepower Flour City tractors were identical, although engine and chassis sizes were different. Many of the largest tractors from around the 1910 era were bought to break sod, either in North Dakota or in Texas, and if they performed well in those areas, the testimonials were used in advertising.

This 40-70 Flour City, the largest model they made, dwarfs the North Dakota men and boys viewing it about 1915. This is just one of numerous models of large Flour City tractors made, which led to the downfall of the company after Owen Kinnard died in 1925. Too many large tractors were being made and too few sold; like a number of other tractor manufacturers who had been successful, the company did not adjust to making smaller tractors—or at least enough of them—soon enough, and in the end run their business disintegrated.

This 40-70 Flour City pulls an 8- or 10-bottom John Deere plow cutting North Dakota sod about 1912. Though it may never be known if Owen Kinnard invented the first tractor, it is obvious from the success of the Flour City line and huge tractors like this that his long experience in the field—some references say he started building a traction engine in 1894—helped him create a very solid tractor.

THE "KINNARD" 15-25

This "miniature" Flour City tractor from about 1912 was a 15-25 Kinnard tractor with a four-cylinder engine. Notice the fuel tank on the left fender of the 15-25. It was improved in 1918, but not enough to keep it in the Flour City line after 1919. The Kinnard tractors were eventually called Kinnard Flour City tractors, and then simply Flour City tractors.

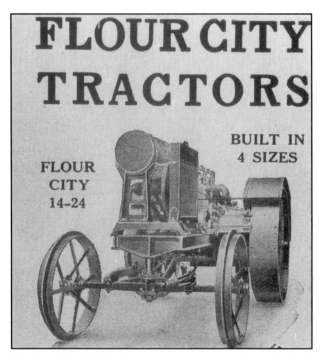

FLOUR CITY TRACTORS

FLOUR CITY 14-24

BUILT IN 4 SIZES

The Flour City 14-24 in this picture was essentially a Flour City Junior that had been improved. It was the last new model made by Flour City.

en a thorough trial before any were put on the market. Already Flour City was beginning with their trademark large rear wheels, as these first ones, which had already been cast in 1899, were five feet six inches in diameter. They would not discontinue the manufacture of the Flour City hay presses, but intended to devote their attention chiefly to the gasoline engine department.

It appears that the first one looked much like the company's portable Flour City gas engine, except for using a chain drive. The new engine merely used their regular engine and adapted it to traction purposes.

Various references dispute the building of the engines, which is why the real first builder of traction engines may never be discovered: one magazine said four of the traction engines were built in 1898, and 28 in 1899. However, another account says Kinnard-Haines made their first Flour City engine in 1897 but did not go into production until 1901.

A 1901 advertisement of the Flour City Gasoline Traction Engine says "it requires no licensed or skilled engineer or fireman. Water tank, team, and fuel entirely dispensed with. Made ready to start in a few minutes. Liability to explode reduced to a minimum."

The Flour City Junior was an oddity, the only two-cylinder Flour City tractor made. It was produced only in 1918. Kinnard claimed that he and Hart-Parr were not really the original inventors of the tractor, but the people who got to the news media first.

This Flour City Junior from about 1915 shows farmers breaking brush land in North Dakota. Kinnard said that just five years previous to this, competition between gas-tractor manufacturers, like himself, and steam-tractor manufacturers was so fierce that the steam people would not allow their tractors to be shipped on the same freight cars as the Flour City tractors. Perhaps the steam people already saw the inevitable, that the gas tractor would displace steam tractors.

Farmers had the unenvious but necessary task of building roads from time to time, as these North Dakotans were doing in this about 1918 photo with a Flour City 40-70 pulling a road elevator. Its common name is a "mucker," and its job is to cut a row of dirt and elevate it up and put it in a pile. A close look near the bottom shows where the road is being built.

In 1910, Kinnard said that there was bitter competition between those who manufactured steam tractors and those who manufactured gas tractors, so bitter that steam manufacturers refused to load their machines on the same freight cars with his gasoline tractors.

In 1915, a Kinnard-Haines circular said of the tractor industry that the tendency seemed to be to make a price that will undersell an established line and to build a tractor to conform to this price. This caused great problems, because established businesses had to lower the prices of their tractors or else risk not selling them; on the other hand, they weren't making great profits, either. With that in mind, K-H said the prevailing small tractor was too small and too cheap, an expensive instrument to those who bought it, and a losing proposition to those who manufactured and sold it. With the advances in price it was still a two-plow affair with a limited capacity in draw bar or belt.

Despite that somewhat bleak outlook, there still was a demand for a small tractor, but Kinnard-Haines felt tractors shouldn't be designed like cars, because the car was different—it traveled mostly on public highways and carried its load on its own wheels, while the tractor traveled mostly in fields and pulled its load, requiring its weight to pull the required load, regardless of how much engine power there was. So it seemed obvious that a small tractor should have not only enough weight to pull a load under ordinary conditions, but extra for emergencies. It was no surprise that K-H then said that their Flour City tractor did exactly that.

In 1918, the company's name was changed to Kinnard and Sons Manufacturing. Seven years later, Kinnard died, and the business never recovered; the decline in heavy tractors also spelled the end of the Flour City line. The company existed until 1929, when it also met its end.

FORD (NOT HENRY)

Henry Ford's success with automobiles was big news in the 1910s, and it seemed only a matter of time before he turned his methods to the farm tractor. Before he got the chance to create a Ford Tractor Company, a group in Minneapolis did. They did have a fellow by the name of Ford in the company, who was undoubtedly hired just for that name. The company didn't build many tractors, though, and the ones that they did were poorly built. But the "Ford" badge on the fender was enough to help this bogus little company make a nice pile of cash.

A group of people from Minneapolis, Minnesota, incorporated the Ford Tractor Company in South Dakota in 1915, and later reincorporated it to the Ford

This Ford Model B had nothing whatsoever to do with Ford Motor Company of Dearborn, Michigan. In fact, the Ford involved in the project knew absolutely nothing about tractors and allowed his name to be used by W. Baer Ewing and several others. It was dark green and had red fenders. The point of naming the tractor was twofold: first, there was no Ford on the market, and the name was a magic name that often guaranteed success. Ford Tractor Company of Minneapolis never claimed it was affiliated with the giant Ford Company in Michigan, but it seemed so by default.

Right
This May 1915 advertisement shows what is probably the earliest model of the Ford tractor, before it went into bankruptcy the next year, and before the second Ford Company was incorporated. Some of the advertisements hinted that this tractor had nothing to do with Ford out of Michigan; in one ad it said "Every farmer needs a 'Ford'," as though to hint that this was not the real thing. The tractors themselves were not very sturdy, so the company probably would not have survived long if the bankruptcy and other legal problems hadn't come along.

This 1916 advertisement shows the 8-16 Ford tractor. One of the distinguishing factors of the Ford advertisements was the dour-looking farmers they used to ride their machines. The machine was listed at $350. The man after whom the machines were really named—one Paul Ford—had something of an attack of conscience when he was accosted by the National Vigilance Committee, who were checking on the validity of the company, said he would sell his holdings in the company for about half of what each share was worth. Many farmers paid $75 down on the Ford tractors with the promise of speedy delivery, but the vast majority of them never saw anything. A local newspaper wrote that, "Everything is in large figures except the cash on hand and in bank."

This 1916 photo shows a Ford tractor, most likely a Model B, running a small separator working in North Dakota. This is one of the very few action photos ever made of the Ford, simply because not many of the tractors were made, and fewer delivered. Because the Ford name was usurped, Henry Ford of Ford Motor Company of Dearborn, Michigan, was forced to name his first tractors Fordsons. After Ford Tractor Company of Minneapolis went out of business, Henry Ford was able to get his name back on his own tractor. This is probably the Model B Ford.

Tractor Company, Inc., in Delaware in 1917. The company claimed that the factory was operating day and night, producing two tractors a day and on the way to five a day. All of this was bogus, as the company only built a very few tractors. How many they sold, however, is another matter.

As quoted from a 1915 newspaper article about The Federal Securities Company, and one of its owners, W. Baer Ewing, "The next exploitation taken up by Ewing and the Federal Securities Company was the Ford Tractor Company. There seems to be a sort of magic in the name of Ford when it comes to doing business with the farmer, and Ewing prepared to take advantage of this fact by taking a young fellow named Carl B. Ford into

the concern and naming it The Ford Tractor Company. The direct statement is not made that there is any connection between the Minneapolis company and the Ford Motor Company of Detroit, but that impression is given by the character of advertising sent out by the company."

In truth, there was nothing illegal about this concept, although many people would question how ethical it was. What was perhaps illegal was how the company did business.

The company was founded on shaky ground, as co-owner Ewing was noted for shady and questionable deals in previous ventures. The major snag was that the company didn't deliver tractors. Farmers paid $75 down for their tractors, and were to pay the rest when the tractors arrived, but even after the down-payments had been made, the tractors didn't arrive, and apparently the company then kept the initial payments. Ewing used his Federal Securities Company as collateral for the Ford Tractor Company, when, as the *Twin City Reporter* says, "Everything is in large figures except the cash on hand and in bank."

Though Ewing might have used questionable methods, Paul (not Carl, as he was named in one paper as mentioned above) B. Ford, after whom the company was named, would not. In a pamphlet put out by the National Vigilance Committee titled "Facts About Advertising of Stock in The Ford Tractor Company, Inc.," members of the Committee tried to contact Ford by going to the plant. Ewing said Ford could not be reached, because he was working at the Ford Experimental Station. However, when the Committee representative left and called by telephone, Ford was immediately available.

"We found him perfectly frank," the pamphlet says, "and willing to answer all questions. He stated that he was a mere figurehead; that he was employed in order that Mr. Ewing might use the name of Ford in the incorporation of his company; that at the time he went to work for Mr. Ewing a man by the name of Kinkaid had practically completed the designing of the tractor (Ewing had claimed that Ford had designed the tractor); that for a time he bore the title of Superintendent of Construction; that on June 16, 1916, he was relieved of his duties, but that he continued to draw his salary; that he only went to the plant when he was called by Mr. Ewing; that the Company did not have any experimental station; that he did not approve in the manner in which the business was conducted, and that he had many times told this to Mr. Ewing; that he was sorry if anybody had been induced to invest any money in the Company on the strength of the name Ford, and if he could find any way to prevent further use of that name, he would do so. Moreover, he offered to sell his holdings in the Ten Million Dollar company at $2.50 a share, although brokers then were quoting the stock at $4.50."

Hugely inflated claims of tractor sales were made, when in truth Ford Tractor Company produced fewer than a hundred of their Model Bs and a second unnamed model. In its quest to rob Peter to pay Paul, Ford eventually had serious cash-flow problems. Everywhere Ford Tractor Company turned, it owed money, so eventually it went into receivership. The property was sold October 21, 1918, by the receiver. The sale included the equipment of the factory in northeast Minneapolis, as well as the company's equity in the leasehold of the property.

It also included stock of material on hand, tractor parts, and all other real and personal property belonging to the defunct corporation.

Disastrous as the Ford Tractor Company story was for many farmers it had a bright side: it provided fuel for a growing fire of resentment by farmers and other Americans in general to do something about scam artists and companies that made false claims, and led many companies to become orphan tractor companies.

GRAIN BELT

Perhaps the Grain Belt Tractor Company should have made beer instead of tractors. Or even run a travel service, for within 18 months of its 1917 startup, the company had headquarters in three (or four, depending on the reference) different cities.

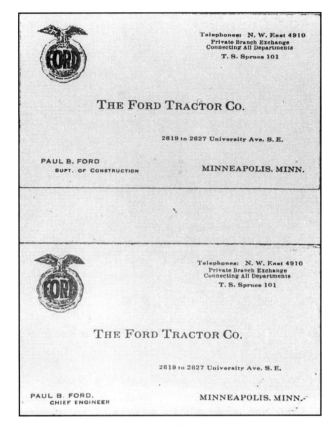

These cards given out by the Ford Tractor Company in Minneapolis variously show Paul B. Ford as Superintendent of Construction and Chief Engineer. In truth, it was just his name that he lent to the company, which did make a "Ford" tractor, but not the tractor that many people perhaps thought they were getting. The company went out of business in 1918 after making very few tractors.

This rare photo of the inside of the Grain Belt Manufacturing Company plant was taken in Fargo, North Dakota, and shows how three gears are cut at the same time. The photo is even rarer when one considers how short a time Grain Belt stayed in any one place. The company was located in Crookston, St. Cloud, and Minneapolis, all of Minnesota, as well as Fargo, North Dakota. *Richard Birklid Collection*

This 1917 ad for Grain Belt tractors plays to the fears of farmers who had been having trouble with dirt wearing away and destroying the gears of their tractors. This 15-30 first built by Grain Belt that year was designed for farmers who wanted a light tractor of medium weight. It ran at 2-2 1/2 miles per hour, depending on the soil it was plowing. It used direct drive from the motor to the wheels, without beveled gears in-between to drain some of the power. It possessed extra-wide wheels—five feet in diameter with an 18-inch face—and all the gears and bearings were in an oil-tight case. *Richard Birklid Collection*

This Grain Belt 15-30 tractor was used at Litchville, North Dakota, in 1917. The bank there had invested a great deal of money in the company (perhaps because it was the only tractor company in the state until Steiger), and lost it all. This single tractor was its payment. It came to Litchville on a flatcar and was unloaded and bought there by an area farmer, who eventually quit using it and put it in his shed. When he decided he wanted to put his new combine in his shed, he removed the Grain Belt, and sold it for junk. *Richard Birklid Collection*

The Grain Belt Tractor Company was organized in Minneapolis, although it appears to have been the brainchild of Charles Himrich, from Fessenden, North Dakota. Another familiar name in tractor circles involved in Grain Belt was Elmer Pitcher of Minneapolis.

It is always curious to see, in the advertisements of the time, information meant to ease the fears of farmers. The ads were designed to soothe farmers who had been bitten time after time by new tractor companies. The ads also include information that is surprising because it's taken for granted today. As in a 1917 ad for Grain Belt 15-30 tractors, which says "The Grain Belt has all working parts running in oil tight housings." Later in the same ad, it says "The transmission has all gears and bearing in oil tight case. The bull pinion and bull gear are also enclosed in oil tight case." And a bit further: "All moving parts are protected from dirt." Dirt had become not only the farmer's greatest ally, but also his darkest enemy when it came to machinery.

The bull pinion on the Grain Belt was made with a square hole which fit on square ends of the differential shaft. This construction was appreciated by those who had been troubled with loose pinions or with those pinions that refused to come off.

Things didn't work out for Grain Belt tractors in Minneapolis, and A.W. Raymond, a former resident of the city, a prominent resident of Wheatland, North Dakota, was interested in the Grain Belt tractor. The *St. Cloud Press* wrote in November 1917 that the value of old time friendship to a city was well illustrated in St. Cloud. The tractor was being manufactured in Minneapolis, but the work wasn't satisfactory, and when the management began looking for a better location, Raymond, knowing St. Cloud and its resources, so strongly recommended St. Cloud that a local firm was employed to make the tractors. Everybody figured the Grain Belt Tractor Company would grow into a big business, because the machine had been thoroughly tested, and was highly touted by experts as "one of the best and most practical on the market, and it is said the demand so far has greatly exceeded the output. Mr. Raymond's many friends here will appreciate his efforts in behalf of the Granite City."

It's not clear in records whether Grain Belt ever actually produced tractors in St. Cloud. But the *Fessenden Free Press* of North Dakota reported in June 1918, "Three Grain Belt tractors were unloaded here the first of the week and two of them were taken immediately, one by Wm. Shaver and one by Andrew Crean, of Bowdon. Mr. Shaver will use the one he bought on his large farm west of town, while Mr. Crean will employ the engine in road grading work near Bowdon. The Grain Belt tractor is the invention of Chas. Himrich, of Fessenden, who, with local men, is now manufacturing and selling these engines from Fargo."

This second rare photo of the inside of Grain Belt Manufacturing Company shows a radial drill in process. Note the tractor wheels in the background. By this time, Grain Belt was making a larger tractor (18-36) than their earlier 15-30, which they began with in 1917. *Richard Birklid Collection*

The Grain Belt 18-36 tractor at work turning sod in North Dakota at the Interstate Fair in Fargo in 1919. Fairs were a huge draw for farmers, and every fair had its machinery hill, where newest models of tractors and other farm machinery were shown off. Grain Belt was no different. Tractor-buyers at this time were getting wary, however, because so many companies had made so many promises and delivered on so few of them.

This 1919 photo of the Grain Belt tractor was taken in front of the company building in Fargo and was perhaps the first one off the assembly line in that city. The company's president, Mr. Prentice, claimed about the same time that demand was so great for the tractor that the company was planning on building a new factory. He said in what was perhaps total honesty that the demand was far greater than the supply, which proved out when only a few dozen of the tractors were ever built.

But cracks had begun appearing in the company. It is almost a sure sign that things are not going well when a company branches out into different types of work only a few months after it had started in an entirely different direction. The company had first been organized in Fessenden, then moved to Minneapolis, then to St. Cloud, and finally to Fargo, where the Grain Belt Manufacturing Company was organized to succeed and combine three different companies: the Grain Belt Tractor Company, The Fargo Foundry and Engineering, and the Dakota Welding and Manufacturing Company. The new business wanted to broaden its field of activities, so they bought a plant at Fargo to give it the first unit of a manufacturing plant that could be enlarged as needed. The Fargo Foundry and Engineering Company manufactured fire fighting apparatus, and the Dakota Welding and Manufacturing Company did a welding and general machinery business. Those undertakings would be continued by the new corporation and the business extended as rapidly as possible.

Another crack appeared in July of 1919, when it was announced the Grain Belt Company was prevented from building a planned new plant by the lack of building materials. Mr. Prentice (President of Grain Belt),

Grain Belt 18-36 tractor at the Interstate Fair at Fargo in 1919. By this time, Grain Belt merged with two other companies. They intended to build products from those companies (fire-fighting apparatus and general machinery, as well as welding).

Gray Tractor Company, existing in that name from 1917 until its demise in 1932, had some of the most beautiful stationery in the business, like this sample. The tractor itself was a most peculiar design. The wide-drum drive allowed farmers to spend more time in the fields during rainy and wet weather than they could with the average tractor, a North Dakota farmer who used one said.

claimed the demand for their product was far greater than the supply, each machine being taken as soon as it is ready to leave the factory.

That may have been true, because very few Grain Belts were built, certainly fewer than a hundred. But within a year, only one thing was true: Grain Belt was dead, and its tractors were orphans.

GRAY

The Gray was in a class by itself. *Northwestern Tractor and Truck Dealer* printed those very words in August 1918, and they became the unofficial company motto. The Gray Tractor was the only tractor that plowed without a stop at the first demonstration at Fremont, Nebraska. The Gray was certainly in a class of its own when it came to looks, a low tractor with a long, full-coverage curved hood.

The Gray seemed to be a solid tractor, and lasted much longer on the market than most of the fly-by-nighters of this era, lasting until the early 1930s. The Gray actually survived tough times which wiped out many tractor companies that had slogged through the great agricultural depression of the early 1920s.

In 1908 W. Chandler Knapp, a prominent fruit grower near Rochester, New York, figured a machine would work better for his orchard cultivation than horses. However, tractors on the market at the time were big steam behemoths that just couldn't fit into the orchards, so Knapp decided to do something about the lack of a usable small orchard tractor: he built one for himself.

He began with a very small tractor he named the Knapp Farm Locomotive. It worked great—under ideal conditions. If the load wasn't centered behind the machine, the tractor was hard to handle; plus it tipped over easily, despite its low center of gravity.

So he redid it in 1909, making it bigger and stronger than the first three-wheeler. Unfortunately, the

rigid frame on both tractors broke. So back to the drawing board for two years of reworking and testing.

The next step involved making a very wide-drive wheel, using two old wheels mounted together. This proved to be the ticket. This machine, built in 1910 and 1911, was more successful. It could negotiate side hills; it was not too heavy for its power, and the frame stood up to

Two models of the Gray tractor were being made when this advertisement was in use in 1920, the 8,000-pound 20-35 Model A, which was selling for $2,150, and the much lighter 5,500-pound Model B, a 15-25 going for $1,650.

its work, all of which had been failings in Knapp's earlier tractors. Also the wide-drive wheel proved very valuable in discing, harrowing, and other forms of light farm work. Thus, this design early proved itself to be workable. From then on, only mechanical difficulties had to be overcome.

One of these was the drive wheel, which got muddied up too easily, and was subject to spoke trouble which was so familiar to all tractor users at the time. It also had transmission and motor difficulties, which were solved in the next two years of testing and refining. The transmission was enclosed instead of left open, the motor put crosswise on the frame, and the wide-drive wheel was changed to a wide-drive drum, without spokes.

At this point, Knapp evidently got more interested in selling tractors than fruit. He moved to Minneapolis, the tractor capital of the world, to build a tractor that would meet the demand of progressive farmers tilling from 160 to 1,000 acres, and who wanted a machine whose use was not limited to plowing, like some other tractors of the era.

In 1914, it was called the Gray Tractor, made by the Gray Tractor Manufacturing Company, and that year earned its reputation of a tractor in a class by itself, by pulling six plows though it weighed only 4 tons, compared to the eight plows pulled by the 10- to 12-ton beasts. In 1916 the Gray sold for $2,250. People recognized that the Gray was a solid tractor by shelling out hard cash for the machines.

In 1918, the company was re-organized and named Gray Tractor Company, Inc. In that year, *Farm Implements* wrote a story headed "Escaped from the Huns

Right
This ad plays on the merits of Gray tractors and their long heritage. Gray made a variety of models that are very difficult to tell apart, including an 18-30 that weighed 6,000 pounds, and an 18-36 that weighed 200 pounds more. The very earliest Grays were much heavier, about 8,500 pounds. The 18-30 was made in 1917 with Waukesha motor and Hyatt roller bearings, and no differential and no bevel gears.

Road builders were especially fond of the Gray tractors because they were so dependable, which prevented the contractors having to pay for work crews that stood around because the tractor had broken down. That's a curious phenomenon when one considers that the tractor was originally invented because the big tractors of the time just before World War I couldn't fit into the orchard, and was originally an orchard tractor, although Knapp tired of orchard work and moved to Minneapolis to start selling his Knapp tractors, which eventually became Grays. The 18-36 was the most popular model built.

The odd-looking Gray tractor was easy to spot with its wide-drive drum, which originally came from having two back tires lashed together to try to gain more purchase in poor soil. The company claimed the use of side arm hitches, which the Gray frame construction lent itself to, doubled the tractor's capacity without increasing fuel consumption, and could be offered by no other tractor. *Minnesota Historical Society*

With Gray Tractor," about a man near Paris who was working on a Gray tractor when the Germans attacked. He drove the Gray off, leaving all his personal belongings, and made the 60-mile trip to Paris without a problem. "Five grays which were being used by farmers in the same section were taken by the Germans," the magazine wrote, "so we will probably later hear that they have adopted this type for their own use as they have done with other successful allied inventions—tanks, aeroplanes, etc."

The Gray Tractor at the time touted in its advertising "Rolling, plowing, harrowing, discing, in one operation." It was a sleek machine.

The wide-drive drum tractor made good roads. "During the six years the Gray Tractor has been upon the market, it has established for itself an unusual reputation for reliability," the Gray literature says. "Its owners have had little trouble from vexatious delays and have seldom been called upon to make repairs and costly replacements." (A number of other tractor companies of the time could have taken hints from the Gray tractor history, noting how it took about six years—1908-1914—of testing to perfect it.)

Because it was so dependable, it was bought "on a large scale" the literature continues, by "real business farmers, Road Contractors, Townships and Counties and during the War it was the standard tractor of the Aviation Construction Squadrons of the United States Army overseas, where it was used for the grading, rolling, and leveling of the aviation landing fields." High praise, indeed.

Road builders especially appreciated the dependability in the Gray, because they couldn't afford to have their work crews lolling about while they paid them simply because their machinery was unreliable. Gray literature talked about all the advantages the tractor had in doing road work.

Other tractor builders could also have taken another cue from Gray: don't make outrageous claims. None of Gray's literature says it is the greatest invention since bread, or that it can increase the number of bushels produced, or do anything grand. It just said it was reliable and it worked.

Gray appears to have been stunned during the agricultural depression of the early 1920s, because a new company was organized in 1925, and the company built the Canadian Special. In 1933 Gray ceased production, probably destroyed by the Great Depression, and joined the list of other orphan tractors.

Chapter Three

Hackney to Huber

Hackney *to* Huber

HACKNEY AUTO-PLOW

The Hackney Auto-Plow, an odd-looking creature of a tractor, had two seats. If you went, say, north, you sat in one seat; if you didn't want to turn the machine around, or couldn't, you just sat in the other seat, flipped a lever, goosed it, and headed south.

The company began in 1901 as Law Manufacturing Company in St. Paul, Minnesota, involving W.A. Law, A.L. Law, as well as the Hackney brothers, L.S. and J.M. Hackney. In 1909, the company name was changed to Hackney Manufacturing Company. At that time, they produced a farm gate, a new line that they had procured.

It's rare that out-of-the-horse's mouth information is available about many orphan tractor companies, but in the case of Hackney, Lucille Howe says her uncles, Leslie, William, and Joseph Hackney, were the inventors of the Hackney Auto-Plow. They were her mother's brothers, better known to many by their initials than by their

This Hackney Auto-Plow was a three-bottom version. It's shown breaking sod in North Dakota about 1918. Despite their odd looks, Hackney Auto-Plows sold very well, because they met the need for a small tractor.

names. Even their parents and six sisters usually referred to them as L.S., W.L., and J.M.

The Hackney's first business venture was as land brokers. They made themselves each a nice nest egg at this, the largest profits resulting from the buying and selling of railroad land in North Dakota. While out there, they realized some other power was needed instead of many horses or big steam rigs to break the prairie and work the large fields of the ranches.

L. S. and W. L. were already inventors of sorts. L.S. patented a device for easy greasing and cleaning of the underside of a car. A frame held the car and tipped it on its side. Evidently the grease pit, however, was more practical.

W. L. also was an inventor, making a gate opener and closer that worked. It was just a simple combination of ropes and pulleys that allowed the user to open and close the gate without getting out of his carriage or car. About the time this invention was put into sale, 1909,

Big Money in Flax

Very likely more money will be made in flax this year than **ever** before. WHY? Shortage in this country and failure of crop **in foreign** countries. Increasing demand and decreasing supply.

At only $2.50 per bushel a low yield of 12 bushels per acre gives a gross return of $30 per acre. This can be done on thousands of acres selling at $20 to $25 per acre.

No Better Opportunity to Make Money and Lots of It

Last year we broke with gas traction engines and seeded to flax over 1500 acres at a cost of 65c per acre. We are now manufacturing the Hackney Auto Plows for this purpose.

We have several thousand acres of splendid flax land for sale and will allow the purchaser of one or more of these Auto Plows to select their land and make the first payment on the land Nov. 1st, 1911, out of the 1911 flax crop, and allow easy terms on the balance.

If you are interested, write us as early as possible for further information. Address,

Hackney Manufacturing Co.

Prior & University Aves.,   **ST. PAUL, MINNESOTA**

This Auto-Plow is breaking sod somewhere in North Dakota in the 1910s. Note the storage area over the single wheel. The Auto-Plow was reversible; the driver could sit facing either direction and drive, which made the machine great for tight spots.

the company became the Hackney Manufacturing Company, but retained all the Laws and Hackneys who had previously been involved.

The aforementioned gate sold so well that they had to increase their capital stock that year. They also made hay tools and sundries, patent gable end door fixtures, litter carriers, hay and stock fixtures, steel lever harrows, steel boss harrows, and hardware specialties.

But their *coup de grace* was the Hackney Auto-Plow, "The greatest labor saving machine on earth today for the farmer," their 1911 advertisements claimed. Howe says the brothers pooled their talents, brought the third brother, J.M., in, and were in business. They began production of the Hackney Auto-Plow on August 1, 1911.

Left
This is the original Hackney Auto-Plow, advertised in 1911 with an offer that the farmer could take possession of the Auto-Plow and pay for it with proceeds from the 1911 flax crop. This edition of the Hackney Auto-Plow is lower slung than later versions. It sold well for the first few years, but eventually its lack of performance caught up with it.

For a few years, it was the cat's meow; Hackney Auto-Plows were sold in the Dakotas, Minnesota, elsewhere in the United States, and even some overseas. Things looked very promising. This seemed to be the normal pattern for many of the orphan tractor companies: a new device was invented, brought into the market, sold well, and the company expanded, before the bottom fell out.

Hackney Auto-Plow Company hoped they would sell 25 units during their first year, into 1912, and when they quadrupled that by April, only nine months later, having already sold 100 machines, they revised their figures and thought they would sell off at least 350 during the first year.

The Auto-Plow was so popular because it was a small tractor that farmers had been clamoring for, as well as being well-suited for farms of average acreage. It was a three-wheeled machine with plows underslung and very compact, made for operation by one man. It could get into fence corners and could work where even a team of horses could not work. It could also add attachments for seeding, discing, harrowing, harvesting, threshing, road grading, orchard work, grinding feed, sawing wood, and so on.

Many Hackney Auto-Plows were sold in the Upper Midwest during the first three years of its existence, but sales tapered off due to other small tractors hitting the market as well as some performance problems. Their first advertising brought 2,358 queries, and subsequent sales required them to triple the size of their factory several times.

Here's a Hackney being driven the "wrong" way; that is, the large wheels on the "back"; advertisements show the Hackney being driven with the large wheels in the front most of the time. All the driver had to do was sit in the second, facing seat, and put the machine in gear and go.

Their advertising brought an avalanche of queries—2,358 of them—and from the original 22 factory workers and three stenographers, expanded to 157 workers and 12 stenographers. To keep up with orders, they tripled the size of their factory several times.

But Hackney hit the old bugaboo of performance. The plow did not always perform as well as the advertising promised. Plus more and more good pull-type tractors were being developed. Sales declined. For only a few short years, the Auto-Plow was manufactured at Prior and University in St. Paul, probably until 1914, when it was sold to Standard Motor Company of Mason City, Iowa. Perhaps a couple thousand were sold all together.

In 1918 disaster struck; the factory burned down. Howe says later she would see the old factory lot full of the unsold Auto-Plows from the window of the streetcar when she attended college in St. Paul.

But that is not the end of the story. Howe says she and her sisters began to look backward as they got older, and took an interest in the family Auto-Plow. In 1977, they finally found a collector in North Dakota who had one of the plows, and arranged to go out and visit it.

This undated early advertisement for Hackney Manufacturing Company of St. Paul shows the variety of items they were building besides the Hackney Auto-Plow tractor. The company was sold to the Standard Motor Company of Mason City, Iowa, in 1914, where it appears to have thrived until the plant burned down in 1918.

"My first impression was its great size. From the street car window, the machines had looked much smaller. Secondly, it looked as new as if it had just come from the factory; the paint was bright, the plow shiny.

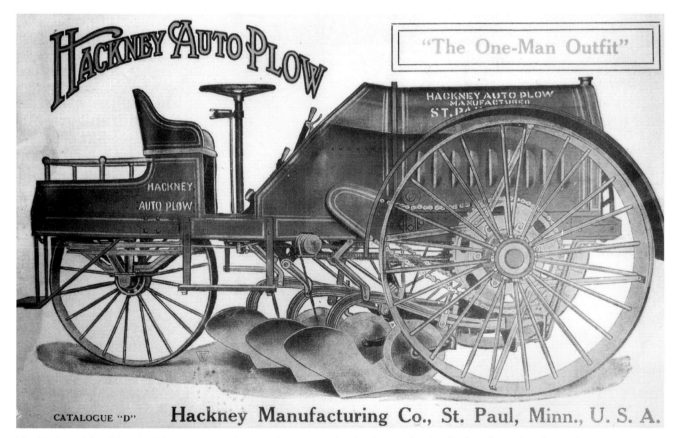

The Hackney "One-Man Outfit" was a nice-looking machine, streamlined and painted red and yellow. Several similar machines came out not long after the Hackney. The Nevada Auto-Plow was one of those machines that closely resembled the Hackney. The Opata Motor Plow and the Graymont also were quite similar to the Hackney.

One of the most surprising things about the Hackney Auto-Plow is its size. It doesn't look that big, but by comparing the size of the people in this photo you can tell how large it is. Another curiosity is that advertisements and drawings of the Hackney always show it with guards around the chain and sprocket (to the right of the driver's leg in this photo) and a fender around the big wheel (the earliest model had a fender that turned into a running board that allowed the farmer to use it to jump up into the seat). Every photo of the machines in the field shows the big-wheel fender and the sprocket gone or removed.

Mr. H. (the owner) explained that it had been in a shed with door and windows boarded shut for many years." They also found one of the original manuals, which allowed Mr. H. to repaint it exactly as it had been.

They even got to drive it. But now, like all these orphan tractors, they exist best, even new and shiny and treated unfairly, in the memories of the people who loved them.

Happy Farmer

The Happy Farmer tractor was simple. L.W. Melcher, chief engineer for the company, summed up the idea at a 1920 Happy Farmer banquet in LaCrosse. "The simpler the machine is made, the stronger it is, the better it is and the more satisfactory it is," he said.

Unfortunately, the meandering path of the companies involved in making the Happy Farmer tractor is not so simple. It began with the Sta-Rite Engine Company, which opened in the LaCrosse can plant in August 1911. Its primary business was making farm engines, and the process of making those engines, though long to explain, is fascinating and an insight into the making of tractors, whether they became orphans or not, everywhere.

An article in the *La Crosse Times* of August 30, 1912, explains, "At the south end of the plant, on the ground floor is the foundry. In this department a score of men are continually working with clay, forming molds which are used for casting the iron parts which are later used in the construction of the engines. All of

the cast iron parts, which are used in the Sta-rite engines, are manufactured in this department.

"In making the molds, several large planks are placed on the floor so as to form a quadrilateral figure, of a size sufficient to contain the pattern to be used. Into this form is placed a fine black sand which is spread about within the form. The pattern is then placed in the

Top right
This Model A Happy Farmer (8-16 horsepower) was offered for $585 during this 1916 advertisement, with the promise that it would go up another hundred dollars by May 5 of the next year. This 3,500-pound machine was guaranteed to pull two plows almost anywhere, although advertisements said it consistently pulled three, with 1,500 pounds guaranteed drawbar pull. One ad said the little tractor repeatedly plowed around all of its competitors, and then pulled them out of the mud. It burned gasoline or, with a special attachment, kerosene.

Center right
The Happy Farmer Model B had not yet come out, although the company was advertising that it would be available June 1, 1917. When it did come out, it was basically a larger version of the Model A. The radiator was mounted parallel to the frame in the B, and across the frame and further back in the A, while the gas tank was obviously larger on the Model B.

Bottom right
Prices were not stable when the 12-24 Happy Farmer Model B was being developed. Before it came out in 1916, it was advertised for $695. By 1917, it was advertised for $735. By 1918, the price had climbed to $1,075 due to the difficulty of getting steel during the war effort. It was also sold about this same time as the LaCrosse tractor. In both cases, the tractor was built around a steel tube instead of a steel girder frame, and contained the only completely water-cooled two-cylinder engine of its time.

The La Crosse
Happy Farmer
MODEL A
8-16 h. p.

$585
F. O. B. LA CROSSE

$735
F. O. B. LA CROSSE

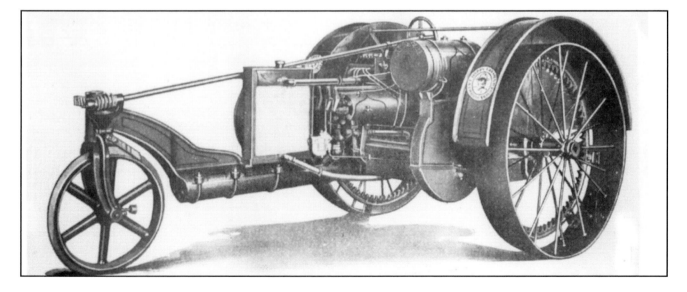

The motto of the Happy Farmer Model H 12-24 was, "Sell one to your enemy and make a friend." All the Happy Farmer tractors were sleek machines that looked like they were ready to work in the field. But all was not happy at the La Crosse Tractor Company; the farm depression of the early 1920s put it out of business.

sand so as to be on a level with the top and the sand is smoothed and packed. Much time and labor is spent on this as it is necessary that the top of the sand be on a perfect level.

"A small quantity of water is then sprinkled along the edge of the pattern in order that the sand may acquire sufficient adhesion to permit the removal of the pattern. A sharp instrument is then stuck into the pattern at short distances and tapped slightly in order to loosen all particles of sand which may have become attached to the pattern. After this, two nails are driven into the pattern and by taking hold of these, it is removed, leaving the design in the bed of sand.

"The work of removing the pattern is the most difficult operation in the making of molds. The molder must be a man of nerve or rather without nerves, as the smallest side movement, when the pattern is being raised, will spoil the mold and hours of labor will have been wasted. It often requires as long as three moments to remove a pattern from the soil and during this entire time, the least unsteadiness on the part of the molder will ruin the mold.

"Occasionally small particles of the sand will cling to the pattern despite all the precaution that can be taken. If the part of the mold which is thus removed is not too large, the sand is replaced by small instruments. This requires the utmost skill. It is often necessary to use mirrors in looking for defects in the lower parts of the molds.

"After the molds are completed molten or liquid iron is poured into them and left to cool and harden. Then the iron is removed from the mold, and sent to the machine shop for finishing."

Happy Farmer Tractor Company was organized in Minneapolis in 1915, using a design for a tractor by William Hartsough, who designed the Lion and one of the Bull tractors, as well as the Big Four tractor, among others. Happy Farmer was perhaps the earliest to stress

Left
In addition to the basic A and B models, Happy Farmer eventually put out a Model F and Model G, both similar to the A and B models. The Model G had a wide-tread front axle. The Model H, as well as a Model M, were 7-12s. While these tractors were being produced, tractor manufacturers were struggling to convince farmers that tractors were useful additions to their farms, although in 1920, B. F. Haney, of the La Crosse Tractor Company, said that he felt the tractor companies were finally winning.

Right
The 1916 Model A Happy Farmer shown in this advertisement had rear wheels 56 inches in diameter with a 10-inch face, and front wheels 31 inches in diameter. It held nine gallons of fuel, and was a mere 5 1/2 feet high, 6 feet wide, and 13 feet long. Its radiator was of an "unusually large capacity," advertising claimed. It also had only two-thirds the parts of the average tractor, which meant fewer mechanical things to go wrong.

King of the Field!

THE LA CROSSE

Happy Farmer Tractor

Model "A"
8-16 H. P.
$585
F. O. B.
Factory

Model "B"
12-24 H. P.
$735
F. O. B.
Factory

The Tractor That Has Made a Distinct Success in the Field in 1916.

THROUGH FOUR FEET OF SNOW—A MINNESOTA MID-WINTER TESTIMONIAL

La Crosse Tractor Co., Minneapolis, Minn.   Bethany, Minn., Jan. 22, 1917.
"Gentlemen: We received the tractor in good shape and had to move same about 3 miles, and the way it crawled over the snow was really a wonder. I had one mile of road where the snow was anything from two feet to four feet deep, and we moved right through on her own power. You can imagine what the roads were as one fellow who just came over the roads offered another fellow $100.00 if he moved that tractor home on her own power; and another fellow (an owner of a HAPPY FARMER TRACTOR) said: 'The HAPPY FARMER will do almost anything but you cannot move that tractor home on these roads'. But I got her there and made the three miles in about two hours."
Yours respectfully,   IWINSKI BROS.

The La Crosse Happy Farmer Superior Line of Tractor Drawn Implements
Will help you to get the cream of 1917 Business

OPPORTUNITY KNOCKS LOUDLY
But Will Soon Cross the Street to Your Competitors—Well?

If you attend the Minneapolis Automobile Show, be sure to visit our display; also call at our office, No. 1203 Hennepin Ave.

Some Good Territory Still Open, But It's Going Fast.

SOME OF OUR DISTRIBUTORS

N. O. Swenson, Inwood, Ia.
City Merc. Co., St. James, Minn.
Ing. Johnson, Hanley Falls, Minn.
Meadows Mfg. Co., Pontiac, Ill.
Hilpert-Moore Machinery Co., Decatur, Ind.
S. A. Bollinger & Son, South Whitley, Ind.
Willis E. Grover, Caro, Mich.
Ohio Happy Farmer Tractor Co., Bucyrus, Ohio.
Bartz Machinery Company, Philadelphia, Pa.
Griffin Motor Company, Mason City, Iowa.

Hathaway Motor Company, Kansas City, Mo.
Machinery Sales Company, Oklahoma City, Okla.
Texas Happy Farmer Tractor Co., Dallas, Texas.
Mathias Grewer, Glen Ullin, N. D.
Leslie Stinson, Grand Forks, N. D.
South Dakota Tractor Company, Watertown, S. D.
T. G. Northwall Company, Omaha, Neb.
Montana Tractor Company, Miles City, Mont.
O. E. Peppard, Missoula, Mont.

Some Good Distributing Territory Still Open—Write Us

La Crosse Tractor Company
Minneapolis, Minnesota

The Happy Farmer logo was a readily-recognizable one and doubtless helped to sell many of the tractors; just the name and the picture can't help but elicit a smile.

safety in some of its ads. Its original cost in 1915 was $550. Some tractors were made in Minneapolis by H. E. Wilcox Motor Company, and advertised as the Happy Farmer tractor, but more were made in LaCrosse, Wisconsin, probably by LaCrosse Implement Company, and were called LaCrosse Happy Farmer tractors. LaCrosse Implement Company had been selling Waterloo Boys, direct competitors of the Happy Farmer, but dropped that line when they began producing their own Happy Farmers.

In 1916, Happy Farmer Tractor Company moved to LaCrosse, and though it seems to have kept its name for a while, finding a new home in the former plant of the Summit Stove works, and the schedule for that year's production called for 2,800 machines, its name and that of LaCrosse Implement Company were combined into the LaCrosse Tractor Company.

There are several similarities between the Happy Farmer and Allis-Chalmers, says C.H. Wendel, tractor historian. Some people wonder whether Happy Farmer copied the design of Allis-Chalmers, or vice versa. The similarities make a person wonder whether at least some of the design of the two tractors originated with a single source.

The LaCrosse Tractor Company of Minneapolis became the selling arm of the Happy Farmer Tractor Company and produced a booklet entitled "A Lesson in Arithmetic," which pointed out the advantage of using a tractor instead of horses on farms. This was one of the favorite topics of the time.

For many modern people this is a tough concept to follow. It seems obvious that a tractor would be much more useful on a farm than horses would be; however, using animals on the farm was deeply ingrained, and though tractors had been on farms for at least a decade when B. F. Hamey, vice president and general manager of the LaCrosse Tractor company, spoke at a banquet of Happy Farmer tractor dealers and wannabes in 1920, he still felt the need to convince them: "The tractor is only on the verge of coming into its own, and results of the inquiries made by the Happy Farmer and results obtained in localities where dealers and farmers were alive to the proposition had conclusively proven that the farmers are going to completely motorize their farms and the tractor will lead motorized farm equipment."

Advertisements for the LaCrosse Happy Farmer Tractor called it the "Perfect kerosene burner," and that it pulled three plows up a 19.4 percent grade without faltering or producing smoke, working on kerosene.

It is always startling how quickly the good, in the tractor industry, can turn into the bad. A headline in the *LaCrosse Times* read, "Tractor Business Growing Apace As Motorizing Comes," on February 24, 1920. A parade wended its way through the LaCrosse welcoming hundreds of Happy Farmer dealers from a five-state area. All seemed to be going well.

Suddenly, the 1920 agricultural depression struck, and Happy Farmer began slipping, just like almost every other tractor company in the United States. Oshkosh Tractor Company was organized to take over the LaCrosse Tractor Company, and built a foundation for their new business before biting the bullet and backing down. Rumor had it in 1922 that the original owners of the business would resume under the name of the LaCrosse Tractor Company.

Perhaps they did, but the results turned out to be nothing. In the early 1920s, one more tractor company turned its tractors into orphans.

Hart-Parr

When you think of the Hart-Parr Company, it is fitting to think of the word "tractor," for they originated the word—or at least were the first company to use it regularly. (Several orphan tractor companies claimed the distinction of having invented the first tractor.)

But you might also think of the word "innovation," for Hart-Parr was top of the line: they developed schools to educate farmers about complicated tractors and machinery they produced; they developed health insurance for their workers; and they sold easy-pay homes and lots to their workforce.

They also built pretty good tractors. In the mid-1890s, Charles W. Hart and Charles H. Parr, young engineering students at the University of Wisconsin, founded Hart-Parr Gasoline Engine Company to build stationary engines.

They had several engine designs and sets of patterns they built up during their courses at the University of Wisconsin. They borrowed $3,000, bought half an acre in Madison, and built a two-story 31x56 building. Hart and Parr finished the building themselves the winter of their graduation. The first two years, Hart-Parr Company lost money, and could easily have closed, as many struggling farm-related companies did over the years. Instead, the stockholders absorbed the losses, and kept the company going. With $3,000 more working capital, the next two years the company made profits, $454.33 and $1,564.16. They were on their way.

Space became a problem as business picked up. They decided to move to a different location in Madison, but real estate was scarce and very high-priced. It was also very difficult to raise money from the people of

Madison. Why? C.H. Parr wrote "They believed it would lessen the desirability of their city as a place of residence." On the urging of Hart's father, who lived in Charles City, they turned to Charles City, Iowa.

After a number of conferences, the business people of Charles City made an offer to the Hart-Parr Company: a building at a very reasonable price, and enough capital to increase the business, if Hart-Parr would agree to transfer their entire manufacturing plant from Madison, Wisconsin, to Charles City, Iowa.

The results were predictable. By Christmas 1901, the deed—and new buildings—were done. Hart and Parr got down to business in Charles City.

The early business of Hart-Parr was based on manufacturing small stationary engines, portable engines, pumping outfits, and wood-sawing outfits. These were vertical type engines with the crankshaft above the cylinder and the crank and open end of the cylinder completely enclosed. They showed remarkably high mechanical efficiency. They also developed oil-cooling for the cylinders, eliminating the cold-weather problems associated with water-cooling.

This 15-horsepower Hart-Parr was probably being tested at Hart-Parr's testing ground near Rudd, Iowa. This tractor appears to be an experimental tractor with perhaps only this single model built. This is also unusual because it had a single front wheel, unlike other Hart-Parr tractors. Rudd, Iowa, was the regular testing ground for Hart-Parr tractors for many years.

Hart-Parr Trainload for One Dealer

In 1926, the Salina Tractor and Thresher Company in Salina, Kansas, sold more than 100 Hart-Parr tractors, and the next year set out to best its previous record. They used territory analysis, advertising, demonstrations, and canvassing, and were so successful that this trainload of Hart-Parrs—40 carloads of 160 tractors—was the result.

This 30-60 Hart-Parr hauling lumber about 1910. The 30-60s were known as "Old Reliables," and were built for a dozen years, with production ending in 1918. Like many of the early Hart-Parr machines, the 30-60 was huge, weighing more than 20,000 pounds, and could trundle in only one forward and one reverse gear not much faster than a horse could walk. The engine was of equally massive proportions, with a 10-inch bore and 15-inch stroke. Nevertheless, it was a popular tractor that did heavy work most satisfactorily.

This made their engine peculiarly adapted for use on the farms in all seasons, and for installation in isolated pumping stations and elevators where adequate care and supervision could not be depended on.

Thus it was easy for Hart-Parr engines to get adopted by elevator lines and farms, blacksmiths, and repair shops. In Charles City, the business grew and expanded very rapidly.

But Hart and Parr were farm boys, and they wanted to invent power machines for large western farms. That happened in 1902 in Charles City, when their first gasoline traction engine was built, and was called a "tractor."

A farmer near Mason City, Iowa, bought the first tractor, and received it in July 1902. He used it for threshing that year, and for a few more years, when he sold it to a neighbor, who continued to use it for threshing and other farm work.

In 1903, Hart-Parr sold 15 tractors. That same year they developed their plowing tractors, and perfected the oil cooling system for them. Suddenly, Hart-Parr tractors were "hot." The company could not make them fast enough.

The first tractor was rated for 17 draw bar and 30 belt horsepower. The 1903 version was a 22-45 horsepower machine. The tractors were massive yet good-looking, their designs heavily influenced by the steam traction engines of the day. They was heavy, with 1,000-pound flywheels in 20,000-pound tractors—Hart-Parr trademarks. Two-cylinder kerosene engines were cooled by oil, and make-or-break ignition systems popped only on demand as the engine load increased or decreased. The tractors were driven and steered by chains and moved at a stately 2.3 miles per hour. Steering required plenty of forethought.

According to a booklet on Hart-Parr tractors from the Charles City Public Library, "This Hart-Parr No. 1 was the first successful production tractor ever built, earning Hart-Parr the recognition as 'founder of the farm tractor industry'."

Hart-Parr went full-time to making tractors. When the price of gasoline skyrocketed, Hart-Parr turned to other fuels. Soon their tractors operated just as efficiently on kerosene or distillate as the more-expensive gasoline.

In 1906, Hart-Parr introduced its 30-60 "Old Reliable," and its advertising manager, W. H. Williams, introduced the first commercial use of the word tractor in promoting Old Reliable, which weighed 10 tons.

Hart-Parr moved upward and onward, with absolutely huge tractors. They built a 40-80 horsepower model, and a monstrous railway-locomotive-sized 60-100 horsepower prairie sodbuster weighing more than 50,000 pounds with wheels nine feet in

This advertisement from 1922 shows the Hart-Parr 30 and Hart-Parr 20, discussing the values of each of them. In the bottom left-hand corner is a reference to the old Hart-Parr No. 1 tractor, built in 1901. Hart-Parr was the first company to use the name "tractor" in referring to their machines, using the name in internal circles in the company in Charles City, Iowa, in 1902. By this time, Hart-Parr called themselves "kerosene tractor specialists." A kerosene-burning guarantee was written into every tractor sale.

diameter. The 60-100 was in Hart-Parr's catalog only in 1911 and 1912.

This tractor was built, Parr wrote, "In obedience to a demand coming from the large western farms that were being developed, and from parties with extensive hauling contracts in the mining regions."

In 1905, plans for one expansion were scrapped, and larger plans made instead—314 feet were added to the machine. The building was fully occupied almost before it was complete.

The company continued to expand, putting up a new 100x100-foot erecting shop in 1906 and the Gray Iron Foundry, the Steel Foundry, and the Power House in 1907. In 1908, Hart-Parr paid its first dividend to its stockholders.

About this time, Hart-Parr expanded, with branch houses at Wichita, Kansas; Aberdeen, South Dakota; and later, Grand Forks, North Dakota; Portage La Prairie,

This 22-45 Hart-Parr from about 1905 was later renamed the 30-60. That year, Hart-Parr scrapped plans to build and expanded their plant, but went to producing tractors full-time. Many farmers worried about the sky-rocketing price of gasoline, so Hart-Parr went to making tractors that would work just as well on kerosene and other distillates.

This 1926 16-30 was a very popular Hart-Parr tractor and one in its lighter-weight series. This was after World War I, when suddenly Hart-Parr found themselves in a quandary because their overseas business, which was substantial, had been cut off in a single stroke. If it had been a lesser company, it would not have survived that blow and the following agricultural depression in the early 1920s.

This about 1905 Hart-Parr came without an oil pump. Instead, they had little drip cups for each piston and main bearing and connecting rod. Chester Reiten, a farmer from near Comstock, Minnesota, had three of these tractors and plowed his several sections of land night and day to the light of a little kerosene lantern hung in front so the operator could see the furrow. At the end of the field, the operator would step down and take the lantern and look behind each drip cup to see if oil was still dripping, before they started back to the other end again. The next year, 1906, when the oil pump for it came out, the farmer bought oil pumps and had them installed.

The year of this 1908 30-60 Hart-Parr run in North Dakota can be identified by the fewer spokes in the back wheel; because of strength problems, more spokes were added in later models. The 30-60 "Old Reliable" was the first machine in which the advertising referred to "tractor" as the name of the machine. Though there is scant proof that Hart-Parr actually invented tractors—several other orphan companies claim that distinction as well—it is documented that advertising manager W.H. Williams was the first to call the machines "tractors" in their advertising for the machine.

Manitoba; and Great Falls, Montana, as well as in other states and provinces. In addition, contracts were entered into with a firm in Buenos Aires, Argentina, as well as Austria and Russia. Shipments were also made to Cuba, Chile, and the Philippine Islands, so that the Hart-Parr product became quite generally known throughout the world.

Now Hart-Parr rethought their mission. Parr wrote, "the company decided that notwithstanding the evident demand for the large machine it was the wrong economic move to produce it. It proved to be too large a proposition to place in the hands of the ordinary unskilled man to operate and care for." Doubtless this concept was fed by the problems farmers were having with the machines on their farms. No one had yet thought of going out into the fields and showing the farmers how to best make use of their machines.

Hart-Parr began a series of instruction programs, in person or by mail. Competitors soon did the same.

Hart-Parr eventually dropped the monster tractors and began making smaller tractors in 1914. The Hart-Parr 15-22 horsepower Little Red Devil was a peculiar tricycle rig. It was propelled by its large single rear wheel, with a direct-drive reversible two-cycle two-cylinder engine. At slowest idle, the timing lever was reversed and the engine would misfire itself into running backwards. At its peak production, Hart-Parr turned out five Little Devils a day, and at $850 each, more than 1,000 sold.

The Little Red Devil was dropped in 1916, partly because the two-cycle engine was extremely sensitive to

This ad for "Old Reliable," Hart-Parr's 30-60 tractor, shows a chart on the side indicating the operating costs of gasoline versus kerosene costs. This ad also discussed their other tractors, the Steel King 40, Oil King 35, Crop Maker 27, Little Devil 22, and "money-making separators."

65

A Hart-Parr 30-60 at some kind of show about 1913. To the left of the John Deere sign is a Flour City tractor.

The Hart-Parr "Little Devil" was Hart-Parr's first venture into the lightweight tractor field. The 15-22 had no transmission or differential. To put the little beast into reverse, a farmer merely had to idle it and throw the timing lever in the opposite direction. It operated at 600 rpm, and had only one rear wheel. The driver of this tractor seemed almost like he was sitting in air, away from the tractor itself. Some people called it the "Little Red Devil."

improper intake mixture or timing. Those incapable or uninterested in keeping the fuel and ignition systems properly adjusted on the Little Red Devil had considerable difficulty with the machine.

Hart-Parr also brought out a rugged, single-cylinder machine designed particularly for service in the building and maintenance of roads. The 35-horsepower tractor soon became the most popular small Hart-Parr, and a great many were placed in the hands of counties and townships as well as individuals for building and maintaining country roads. They contributed a large share to the great improvement in the dirt roads of the Middle West.

Hart-Parr also thought of what was best for its workers. Housing had become a problem, so Hart-Parr bought houses, as well as a tract of land divided into lots, and rented them or sold them on the easy-pay program to Hart-Parr workers.

Hart-Parr also began the Hart-Parr Relief Organization, which furnished employees with health and accident insurance at a moderate cost. The company bore all the office expense and contributed 20 percent of its assessments. The program was dropped when national companies began providing accident and sickness insurance.

Hart-Parr also donated to building a YMCA and the Charles City Western Railway Company. By 1914, Hart-Parr grew enough to require reorganization.

Then came World War I. "Almost in one day," Parr wrote, "the extensive foreign business of Hart-Parr Company…was cut off completely." Hart-Parr lost more than $100,000 owed them in those foreign countries.

Hart-Parr eventually also manufactured its own equipment to make war materials, because the equipment they needed could not be gotten anywhere else, due to demand. Hart-Parr also made washing machines.

In 1918, Hart-Parr introduced two practical smaller tractors, the 15-30 Type A, and the New Hart-Parr 12-25. In 1919, Hart-Parr sold out to their partner, C. D. Ellis, but continued working for the company.

Eventually Oliver Chilled Plow Works bought Hart-Parr, and continued producing Hart-Parr tractors. The first Oliver-Hart-Parr was introduced in 1930, the 18-28. Hart-Parr quickly adopted rubber tires, and in 1932, pneumatic tires replaced the hard rubber. Hart-Parr also introduced its spider-web-like "tiptoe" steel wheels.

Soon the Oliver logo became larger than the Hart-Parr, and in 1938, one year after C. W. Hart died, and three years before C. H. Parr died, the name Hart-Parr disappeared forever from the name of tractors.

This 1912 Hart-Parr 30-60 shows how versatile the machine was, as it is being used for threshing in North Dakota, an expected job for a machine of its size.

The Hart-Parr 18-36 weighed 6,250 pounds and had a 251-cubic-inch engine. The company claimed it developed 43 horsepower on the belt and 32 horsepower on the drawbar, a surplus of 79 percent above its rating. They also claimed it would cut a farmer's farm power costs in half.

Heider

The Heider Manufacturing Company of Carroll, Iowa, was founded by a group of men that included John Heider, who farmed in Iowa for 30 years before going into the tractor manufacturing business, his son, Henry Joseph (H. J.), who seemed to be the brains of the outfit, at least in terms of inventions and patents, and Joseph Conrad (J. C.) Heider.

Heider is unique because it is a business that still operates today, making smaller farm equipment like wagons, although the tractors have been orphaned. Also, early Heider tractors had a gasoline engine starter which switched to kerosene after the engine became warm enough to operate. Add to that the fact that the Heider tractor people got out of the business when it started getting too big for them, instead of starting to invest heavily in a risky venture, and you have an unusual company.

The first Heider tractor was a small one by the standards of the day, weighing only 4,500 pounds, compared to others that weighed four and even five times that much. Heider's first tractor model was announced in July 1911, and sold for $1,300.

After the second Heider came out a year later, business picked up, perhaps because of some major changes were made on the tractors. The cooling fan on the open radiator disappeared, probably because the cooling was sufficient from evaporation without the use of a fan. The belt pulley and friction drives were moved ahead of the bull pinions, and the canopy was improved. Along with fenders, all these additions increased the sales appeal. A short time later, Heider Mfg. Company contracted with Rock Island Plow Company, a power of the time in farm implements, to sell Heider tractors teamed with the well-known Rock Island Plow. An ad of the time says, "What other tractor gives you the guarantee of service that the Heider gives you....Heider success is due to its performance—year after year—in every soil—on every power job. Let the Heider owners tell you. You don't have to take a 'demonstration' as your assurance."

This Heider belongs to John Thompson of Barnesville, Minnesota. This 12-20 used a heavy-duty Waukesha motor and was touted as having no gears to strip, because it was friction-driven. The Heider tractor was a well-made and well-thought-of tractor, which makes it seem odder that the original company owners decided to get out of the business just when things were starting to pick up.

This "little" Heider from about 1916 had a 15-horsepower rating and was pulling a disk in a North Dakota cornfield. By this time, the Heider owners had decided they didn't want to risk making the company larger, which they would have had to do because of increased sales, and so they sold out to Rock Island Plow Company, to which they had been teamed selling Heider tractors and Rock Island Plows. *Richard Birklid Collection*

This Heider is plowing a North Dakota field in 1920. Heider tractors operated with a variable-speed friction drive. They possessed a large disk with seven notches in it, and the further the farmer pulled a friction wheel up on the disk, the faster the tractor went, spinning the transmission faster. It went between 2 and 5 miles an hour, but one North Dakota farmer said you could slow it down so far that it was almost not moving at all. Speeds could be varied by putting the friction wheel between the notches too. The same worked for reverse direction. *Richard Birklid Collection*

Heider tractors were pretty, with red wheels and lime-green bodies accentuated by red stripes and greenish-yellow stripes. They were powered by Waukesha four-cylinder 4.50x6.75 inch engines.

Heider seems to have had some pull as a company, because an article in *Farm Implements* in 1917 talked about how American soldiers were studying the Heider tractor, as a number of them had been purchased by the government for use overseas. They were to make a careful study of the Heider tractor before they were shipped overseas, where their experience would be of practical value as many Heider tractors had been shipped to the various allied countries for war purposes and these are the men who would be called upon.

Heider engines were four-cylinder units, which were somewhat unusual at the time. Also, the entire engine moved forwards and backwards when gears were changed to increase speed.

But no matter the innovations or how well the Heider tractors were selling, the Heider family decided that it was too much for them. When they could no longer handle the manufacturing in their small plant, they sold the Heider line to Rock Island Plow Company in 1915. For a dozen more years, the Rock Island Plow Company made and sold Rock Island Plow Company Heider tractors. Production continued until 1927, when after an unknown number had been made, the tractor met the fate of hundreds of other orphan tractors.

HUBER

One of the overlooked facets of builders of early tractors was their creativity. Few were more creative than Edward Huber of Marion, Ohio. Energetic, inventive, and far-seeing Edward Huber and his friend, Lewis Gunn, formed a partnership in 1870 to manufacture a revolving hay rake and other light farm equipment Huber had developed and patented, and to operate a planing mill. These were to be the first of more than 100 different items that Huber patented.

Huber, Gunn and Company gave way to Huber Manufacturing Company. For most of the years while Huber operated the manufacturing company, he had his fingers in a variety of different manufacturing pies in Marion.

Huber invented a steam farm engine and a grain thresher, and then for the next 20 years steam traction and portable engines and grain threshers were the principal products of the new corporation.

In 1894, Huber introduced a Gasoline Traction Engine. Originally, it was to replace the steam engine in

This 1922 advertisement shows that two types of Heider tractors were sold at this time, a 12-20 and a 9-16, by the Rock Island Plow Company. Due to the lack of clutch, transmission gears, or bevel gears because of the friction drive, the Heider had about 20 percent fewer parts than other tractors, which meant less to break down, but also fewer parts to push the power through, and less vibration. *Richard Birklid Collection*

In about 1913, Heider lowered the price for their 5,000-pound, eight-foot-high second tractor $400, to $995. The company said the price drop was a result of increased production.

This 1915 advertisement shows the 10-20 HP Heider for $995. By this time the Heider family had gotten out of the making of tractors because the business had grown too quickly, and they weren't interested in taking a big chance and expanding. The Heider was the result of John Heider's 30 years of farming before he went into the tractor business. Heider company claimed the friction drive on their tractors was conceded to be one of the greatest features ever built into a tractor because there was less chance for trouble and no gears to strip.

The 20-horsepower Huber return-flue traction engine in the picture has square wheel spokes, which helps differentiate the Hubers from the Minneapolis line, although by the sign it is clearly a "New" Huber. The Huber steam traction engines were designed for general farm work, and thus could easily handled by anyone who had a concept of steam power.

This 20-horsepower Huber steam roller, or road roller, was used to make roads about 1917. Road-making was a sometimes unpleasant and time-consuming but necessary part of a farmer's life. This machine was a single-cylinder that was heavy enough to compact crushed stone or gravel. When tearing up old streets to resurface them, a scarifier was added behind the machine to break up the old material so a road grader could more easily handle it.

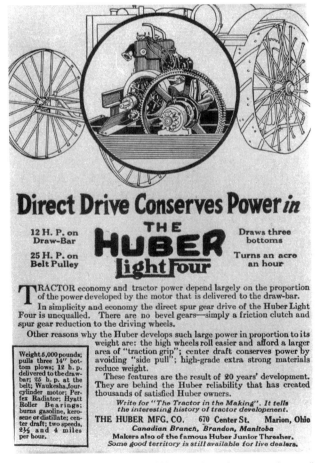

Direct Drive Conserves Power in
THE HUBER Light Four

12 H. P. on Draw-Bar
25 H. P. on Belt Pulley

Draws three bottoms
Turns an acre an hour

TRACTOR economy and tractor power depend largely on the proportion of the power developed by the motor that is delivered to the draw-bar.

In simplicity and economy the direct spur gear drive of the Huber Light Four is unequalled. There are no bevel gears—simply a friction clutch and spur gear reduction to the driving wheels.

Other reasons why the Huber develops such large power in proportion to its weight are: the high wheels roll easier and afford a larger area of "traction grip"; center draft conserves power by avoiding "side pull"; high-grade extra strong materials reduce weight.

Weight 5,000 pounds; pulls three 14" bottom plows; 12 h. p. delivered to the draw-bar; 25 h. p. at the belt; Waukesha four-cylinder motor; Perfex Radiator; Hyatt Roller Bearings; burns gasoline, kerosene or distillate; center draft; two speeds, 2½ and 4 miles per hour.

These features are the result of 20 years' development. They are behind the Huber reliability that has created thousands of satisfied Huber owners.

Write for "The Tractor in the Making". It tells the interesting history of tractor development.

THE HUBER MFG. CO.   670 Center St.   Marion, Ohio
Canadian Branch, Brandon, Manitoba
Makers also of the famous Huber Junior Thresher.
Some good territory is still available for live dealers.

This 12-25 Huber weighed 5,000 pounds and was rated to pull three 14-inch plows. The Waukesha four-cylinder motor burned gasoline, kerosene, or distillate and the transmission had two speeds, 2 1/2 and 4 miles per hour.

providing power for threshing machinery. Huber is generally credited with being first to put a gas tractor in production on a commercial basis.

These tractors were lumbering giants. Magnetos, carburetors, and spark plugs had yet to be developed, streamlining was unheard of, and ease of operation had not become a vital engineering detail.

About the turn of the century, Huber bought the VanDuzen Company of Cincinnati, and built a couple dozen of single-cylinder traction machines, but was not satisfied with them. He kept designing, until 14 years later he finally came up with a tractor that he felt he could sell.

In 1908, Huber introduced the Steam Roller, which was a Huber steam traction engine with a heavy roller taking the place of the front wheels, and with extra-wide rear wheels. In 1920, the one-man-operated Huber Maintainer was introduced. Huber's Automotive Type Motor Roller introduced in 1923 "revolutionized the road construction industry here and abroad," a history of the company says.

Huber Steam Traction Engines hold a strong place in the hearts of many people. A 1914 Huber was used until 1958, when it was restored. It was used until the 1970s when the State of Minnesota ruled that lap seam boilers over 36 inches in diameter could not operate.

This didn't stop the collectors loyal to the Huber brand. They pushed for an easing of the restriction, and after very extensive testing of the thickness of the boiler plate and an X-ray of the seam, the engine was pronounced steam-worthy.

Huber made a variety of other tractors very successfully into World War II, when the company was requested to concentrate production on Huber's 6-, 8-, 10-, and 12-ton three-wheel Road Rollers. During the war they were seen in Africa, Egypt, India, the far Pacific, and throughout Allied Europe, wherever roads and airfields were constructed.

By 1948, Huber tractors had become only figments of tractor collector's dreams, and one more set of orphans. Perhaps it was just too difficult to retool all the machinery again, or compete with new tractor companies on the market.

Huber still exists today, manufacturing construction equipment.

The Most Powerful Tractor at Its Price

NOW comes a new Huber tractor that has just hung up new records of power and economy in two great State University tests—Ohio and Nebraska. It is the most powerful tractor of its weight and the most economical tractor of its power.

The Huber Super Four is sold as a 15-30 tractor at a 15-30 price, but it actually develops 50 per cent more than this rating.

At the Ohio State University test it showed a maximum belt pull of 46.17 H. P. constant run at rated speed. The fuel economy at rated load was a new record for four-cylinder engines. At the Nebraska test (official figures soon available) the results were substantially the same with a corresponding drawbar pull.

Hook this tractor to a 28x48 separator and you have a real threshing outfit with as much capacity as the medium sized steam rigs. The complete outfit costs but little more than the price of the steam engine alone. A steam engine renders but little service except for belt work. The Super Four not only furnishes a steady, dependable power for threshing but it pays its way every month in the year doing all kinds of heavy field and belt work. It pulls three plows in any soil as easily as other three-plow tractors pull two. Great power, high wheels, short turning radius and speed make it unequalled for road work.

Write for booklet "Power"

For those who want a smaller outfit, the Huber Light Four
and the Huber Jr. Thresher fill the bill

The Huber Manufacturing Co., 670 Center St., Marion, Ohio

Dealers: Here's a tractor that will sweep the field at its price. Some excellent territories still available.

This Super Four Huber was a 15-30 tractor, as the advertising said, sold at a 15-30 price, but it developed 50 percent more than that rating (46.17 horsepower constant-run belt pull at an Ohio State University test). Fuel economy was also good; the company claimed it set a new record for a four-cylinder engine.

This Huber Light Four was made by Huber for the first time in 1917. The Light Four's 5,200 pounds was quite light when compared to the 24,000 pounds of the 18-horsepower Huber steam traction engine. This half-side view of the Light Four shows one of its most distinguishing features, the huge front wheels.

Huber also made threshers, like this Huber Supreme, which it "paired" with the Super Four in advertisements. The Huber Jr. Thresher was also recommended for use with the Super Four, rather than paying a custom person to do the grain and taking the chance that the grain would remain in the field too long, stay wet, and sprout, or shell out when it was too dry. Huber also said they would be glad to send out information on how to organize a threshing association.

The Huber Supreme In Steel

Now the Huber Supreme Thresher can be had in all steel construction.

No separator ever offered the American thresherman has a better record for reliability, easy running, and big capacity for its dimensions than the Huber Supreme.

It can be operated in custom work with a moderate sized farm tractor—saving fuel and water hauling, making better time on the roads, setting up quicker

and making more money for the thresherman. The new steel type is all roller bearing equipped. It threshes marvelously clean.

A Huber Supreme and Huber Super Four tractor is the most profitable equipment any thresherman can buy. It will pay for itself quicker and make more money.

Get description and prices on this new steel thresher. You can have it in wood if you prefer. Write us now.

The Huber Manufacturing Co., 122 Center St., Marion, O.

TRACTORS · SINCE 1898 · **HUBER** THRESHERS · SINCE 1879 ·

Above
The 30-60 Huber first came into the world in 1912. This machine
is owned by Sid Bayliss, of Fargo, North Dakota. It's distinctive for
its large tubular radiator. Huber tractors were found all over the
world during World War II

Left
This 1916 Model 35-70 cleared $2,100 for a South Dakota farmer
in 50 days, he declared. Huber claimed that with this tractor, two
men could do the work of 10 or 12 men with less efficient equipment. Huber claimed it was the biggest tractor value in the world
at that time.

Chapter Four

Keck-Gonnerman *to* Little Giant

The Kay-Gee 30-60 tractor made by Keck-Gonnerman was called a Model N and was the largest made by Keck-Gonnerman.

KECK-GONNERMAN

The Keck-Gonnerman company was begun in 1873 by John C. and Winfield Woody, and John Keck entered the business in 1877. John Keck was known to be tireless, frugal, and honest. A series of other partners and owners culminated in the addition of William Gonnerman and Louis H. Keck. In 1901, it was incorporated as the Keck-Gonnerman Company. It was the outgrowth of a small foundry business.

Early lines included threshers, portable saw mills, and engines. In 1904, coal mining machinery was added. By 1913, Keck-Gonnerman had enjoyed a steady and satisfactory growth, with high-quality products marketed throughout the United States, while its officers were among the successful men of southwestern Indiana.

Their first traction engines were side-mounted single-cylinder engines that were very simple and powerful. They were well-balanced and had everything to make a good traction better. The traction clutch was positive and was one of the best found on any traction engine. A Keck-Gonnerman hooked to a good thresher would make itself known.

In its early days, Keck-Gonnerman was an innovative company, and, in 1917, it realized its huge steam traction engines had become passé, so they moved into the gas tractor business, although they continued making the steam traction engines until the late 1920s. Keck-Gonnerman gas tractors were as well-made as their steam traction cousins.

Keck-Gonnerman had a solid reputation from the building and operation of its threshers, sawmills, and steam engines. This reputation would carry over into their gas engines, making it easier for the company to market a new gas tractor.

Their first tractor, the 12-24, closely resembled Aultman-Taylor tractors and caused confusion among buyers. Perhaps that's why Keck-Gonnerman modified the tractor, called it a 15-30, and dropped its price by some $600 by 1923. As an option, a cab could be purchased for $25, and extension rims could also be purchased at $10 per inch of width per set, or $50 for rim extensions five inches wide.

In 1920, more than 100 tractor companies existed, and during that same year the agricultural depression set in, and practically every tractor company organized during the previous 10 years died of lack of capital. Keck-Gonnerman was able to weather that storm, doubtless due to solid financial methods. Keck-Gonnerman's solid reputation was also a factor.

In 1928, Keck-Gonnerman took a bold step: they announced a new and modern line of tractors, called the Kay-Gee line. This line and the active part of the Keck-Gonnerman tractor industry lasted through 1937, although tractors were actually sold through World War II, and into 1946.

In about 1930, the steam-drive–Keck-Gonnerman plant was converted to electricity. The *Western Star* newspaper wrote, "Owing to the large amount of orders now on hand at this plant, the work of changing the power is going on slowly at present, as it is necessary that production keeps pace with the orders received. A portion of the machinery is now being electrically driven and gives entire satisfaction." The company installed its own dynamo, and retained its old steam boiler for use in the new plant. The plant occupied four city blocks.

Some of the Kay-Gee line came and went, like the 25-50, manufactured only between 1928 and 1930. Their largest, the 30-60, weighed five tons, sold for $3,000, and was very popular with sawmill operators. They liked its great power, and yet it was easier to operate than a lot of other tractors, especially those that had been made earlier.

During the 1937 flood of the Ohio River, Keck-Gonnerman provided steam engines to pump water for the city. By this time, the company's products had reached all over the United States, as well as Canada, Mexico, and Uruguay.

Sometimes it's difficult to tell why a tractor company went belly up, and in the case of Keck-Gonnerman, it is even more difficult. Perhaps the Great Depression had something to do with it (although from 1937 to 1946 tractors were sold, but business was not solicited). All reference material about K-G seems to stop discussing the company in the 1930s, before it quit making tractors.

About 300 people worked at K-G during its heyday, making thousands of tractors all told, but today all that remains of the once great and venerable

tractor company are its orphans, and the Keck Motor Company, a car dealership.

LAUSON

John Lauson was a representative of what the power of one word and one man can do not only in a city—New Holstein, Wisconsin—but in an entire industry.

John Lauson was born in 1868 to a family of Schleswig-Holstein German immigrants who were highly skilled, true artisans, expert craftsmen—people of vision of many skills and professions. Among the skilled craftsmen who helped establish the new community of New Holstein were the five Lauson brothers. They brought to America and the community a tradition of craftsmanship—an inborn sense of "know-how" that they had inherited from their fathers, and were to pass on to their American-born children.

One of those children was John Lauson. His father, H.A. Lauson, died in 1882. Suddenly, John Lauson, at age 14, had to become a man. He took over his father's responsibilities in the Lauson Brothers Implement Company, a small implement and repair shop. Two years later, at the tender age of 14 and in full partnership with his uncle George Lauson, and J. H. Optenberg, they started a new machine repair shop, using only windmill power. A year later the shop was destroyed by fire, then reorganized as John Lauson, H.

Right
This Lauson 1920 advertisement shows its standard 15-30. The standard 15-30 was about two tons lighter than its sister 15-30 road model, which had cast iron rear wheels. Lauson published some wonderful tractor catalogs, including one for the 15-30 that was touted as "a picture book" of power farming. Each page carried a different power farming scene, along with essential information in bold type.

Optenberg and Company, with $50 worth of stock. The plant specialized in the repairing of steam tractors, widely used at the time for threshing.

They also manufactured heavy steel items like boilers and smoke stacks, which led them eventually to making steam traction engines, their first standardized product called The Uncle Sam (not to be confused with the Uncle Sam Tractor Company of later years). The company built 25 of the Uncle Sams before John Lauson bought Optenberg out in about 1896, and renamed the business John Lauson Mfg. Company. John Lauson immediately dropped the manufacture of steam traction engines, and set his plant to concentrating on steam boilers, varied sheet metal products, and heavy machinery repair. This variety of enterprises within the compa-

Left
This 1925 ad shows a picture of a Lauson 15-30, but also mentions their two earlier efforts that introduced Lauson to the tractor field, the 12-25 and 20-35. It used its own Lauson engine for power, like all the Lauson tractors.

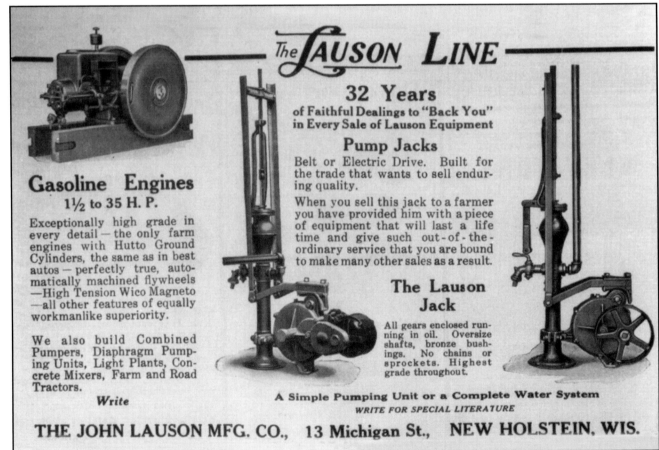

Lauson sold other equipment while they made their fine tractors, as this ad shows. The legacy of the Lauson company, and especially founder John Lauson, was that one person could make a huge difference. Lauson was credited with single-handedly creating and changing the community of New Holstein, Wisconsin.

THE HIGH POWERED

LAUSON 12-25
DUST PROOF—ALL GEARS ENCLOSED

Just what the farmer wants and at a price within every farmer's reach

A light weight three-plow tractor with gears enclosed and operating in oil. A 12-25 tractor that develops around 24 horse power at the drawbar and over 37 horse power at the belt. In reality a 20-35 tractor with a 12-25 rating and price.

It is the established reputation of Lauson products that is increasing the demand for Lauson Tractors today— a reputation built on actual performance in the field. Even during present depressing farm conditions, farmers are realizing that the Lauson Tractor is highly essential and necessary to receive the full benefit of their original investment in the farm.

Write for complete information on tractors and on 1½ to 30 horse power Lauson gasoline and kerosene engines.

THE JOHN LAUSON MFG. CO.
113 Monroe St.   New Holstein, Wis.

For heavier work on farms or on road jobs, the 15-30 or 20-35 horse power Lauson Tractor is highly adaptable.

The Lauson 12-25 did well in its Nebraska test, with actual drawbar horsepower of 24 and 37 horsepower at the belt, the company claimed. They said it was in reality a 20-35 tractor being sold at a 12-25 price. Lauson built some of the better quality orphan tractors.

The LAUSON 15-25

DUST PROOF
ALL GEARS ENCLOSED

THE evolution of farm power from the ox team of the early settler to the tractor of the modern farmer has taken place within the last eighty years.

¶ Since the introduction of the first tractor, there has been constant evolution within the industry itself, the final manifestation of which is that powerful, economical, efficient farm power unit, the Lauson "Full Jewel" Tractor.

¶ In this tractor are combined all the features that make for tractor perfection. Experts who are "tractor wise" regard the Lauson as the pattern tractor—the standard of the tractor industry.

¶ In the following pages we give some of the vital construction details which go to build up Lauson quality. They indicate the necessary features you should look for when judging tractor worth and capacity.

¶ Owing to increased production, we are ready to consider connections with high grade dealers in territory where we are not now represented. If, after a study of the following pages, you believe you can qualify for the Lauson organization, write to us for full particulars. We have a powerful co-operative sales plan to assist you.

THE JOHN LAUSON MFG. CO.

185 Monroe Street
New Holstein
Wisconsin

EVOLUTION OF FARM POWER

Lauson claimed their 15-25 kerosene tractor was five years ahead of its time, and delivered a liberal surplus of power for those tough jobs. Like Volkswagen many years after them, they claimed that this "patterned tractor" had not changed in three years, and that was one of its strength. Perhaps they were right; along with the 20-35, the 15-25 took 17 firsts at the National Plowing Contests.

ny was to be a trademark of the company, but all based on one word: quality. Or craftsmanship, if you will. As the years passed, the company gained a solid reputation for quality products that extended worldwide.

Repairing old steam boilers was difficult work. Usually the boiler under repair was one of a set of two or three, two being in use while the third was being repaired. Was it hot? So hot, that electric light cords being used on the job frequently caught fire! So hot, that when electric cords could not be used, the candles used in their place inside the boiler quickly degenerated to an unshapely mass of tallow! After this hot, hard work, the

employees went out to "scorch" the city streets and nearby country roads on their bicycles.

About the middle 1890s, plans were laid for the first Lauson Gasoline Engine, called the Lauson Frost King, to be used on farms for various work. Again, the quality was outstanding. The first one made was hooked up to be used in the plant.

In 1915, John Lauson was one of the first to jump into the manufacture of tractors. He also purchased the Alyward Foundry company to make his own castings.

The company started with two tractors, a 15-25 and a 20-35. Quality? In 19 starts at the National Tractor Pulling Contests, the company won the contest 17 times, a remarkable feat for an established tractor company, absolutely incredible for an upstart company new into the business.

Like many other companies of the time, the Lauson Company tractors kept some features just for the

Left
The farm power booklet was a unique idea from the Lauson company. This is the cover of the 15-25 booklet. Inside were separate drawings of power farm situations, along with directions on how to run tractors.

sake of nostalgia; the cab was a canopy-type hood that looked much like those on horse-drawn buggies.

The next few years were difficult years for tractor builders, as hundreds of models came onto the market, fizzed out, and died away. But the quality of the Lauson tractors kept them alive and prospering. New Holstein began to call itself "Home of Quality." Ads touting Lauson tractors also talked about the "super quality" of their tractors.

Curiously enough, one of their ads from the late 1910s offered "rebuilt and second-hand tractors and engines," in a listing below the ad for their Lauson 16-32 tractor. They sold rebuilt Lauson tractors, all 15-25s (two in A1 condition, one in good, and one in fair); as well as tractor bargains, which included a Case 60 horsepower steam traction engine, and a Rumley Oil-Pull 16-30, "cheap."

John Lauson was a curious man. He was a gruff, rough-and-tumble man who made huge and powerful iron machines, but he had a heart of platinum. Even

Sensation!

Here's the sensation among tractors—it weighs 5775 lbs. *yet it easily pulls four 14-inch breaker bottoms.*

At Minot, N. D. Tractor Demonstration it pulled four breaker bottoms in raw prairie, without a stop.

Durable!

A Liberty Tractor the first one built—has plowed approximately *1000 acres without breaking a single part or needing any repairs!*

Made of best materials—roller bearings—lightest running—a man can easily move it along the floor by hand—no exposed gears—all working parts run in oil.

A Seller!

If you want a handsome profit, if you want to get the most desirable tractor business and satisfy farmers who want the best, if you want to avoid excessive service costs, don't make any connection until you know all about the Liberty. Write or wire us at once.

The Liberty Tractor Co.

316 North Washington Ave. Minneapolis, Minn.

Light Weight

High Grade

Four Cylinder

Four Plow

Kerosene Tractor

Practically no Breakage or Repairs

A Better Tractor

The logo for the advertising of the Liberty Tractor makes the tractor look like it is an official tractor approved by the U.S. Government. Since the tractor was being sold during World War I, government powers were concerned about the use of the name "Liberty" because government trucks used during the war possessed that same moniker.

as head of what came to be a large company, he went out into the plant and worked on the lines with the men, who simply called him "John." He loved the outdoors, and when flowers started growing in early spring, he took orphans and other children of the area out into the swamps to pick the flowers. When he died unexpectedly on April 15, 1922, his obituary ran half of the front page of the New Holstein Reporter. "When the early spring flowers peeped forth from mother earth," says the paper, "Mr. Lauson would load up his big automobile with children, and go to the swamp or woods where great armsful of flowers would be gathered. He enjoyed these annual pilgrimages as much as any of the children.

"He was of sterling character, just, upright and outspoken but ever ready to help those in need. Enemies had he none, among his associates, fellow citizens or competitors. He was beloved by all..." A huge crowd gathered at the railroad depot when his body was brought back from where he had been visiting.

That same obituary credited him with "virtually creating an entire community" of New Holstein. "It can be truthfully said," the obituary continued, "that 'none knew him but to love him'."

His death did not mean the end of the company; it went on strong for another decade. But the farm depression, and eventually the Great Depression, sucked the wind out of the Lauson Company. The company had given too many farmers too much credit for their tractors and the company went bankrupt in 1935. It came back in different form, selling small engines once more, built itself up, and was eventually purchased by Hart-Carter of Peoria, Illinois, and eventually sold to Tecumseh Products Company in 1956.

In the end run, thousands of quality Lausons were built, but the quality probably only delayed the death of the company.

LIBERTY

Like the Ford Tractor Company that wasn't Henry Ford, the Liberty Tractor Company ended embroiled in controversy over the company name. In this case, the name got the company in trouble because of several other companies using the same name. The fact that one of the "companies" was the U. S. Government didn't help matters.

Liberty Tractor Company was organized in 1917, by Elmer Pitcher of Minneapolis, and two North Dakotans, Paul Hans and Emil Pipe, of Davenport, North Dakota, although the company was not incorporated for more than another year.

However, the 1917 date proved crucial when Associated Advertising Clubs wrote a May 2, 1918, letter that said, "As you know, the name 'Liberty' is applied to the new government motor as well as trucks which are being used by the government in the war. We are wondering on what basis this apparently privately-owned tractor concern is making use of the phrase 'Liberty Tractor'." Enough bad things had happened in advertising in the tractor industry that people were trying to clean it up, and jumped at what seemed the slightest infraction.

The Minneapolis Advertising Forum wrote Liberty Tractor Company, and Elmer Pitcher, the manager, answered, "We have not as yet put any tractor on the market, we are only getting some out for tests. We have no stock on the market. We adopted the name 'Liberty' October 21, 1917."

Further checking determined that McVicker Engineering Company designed the tractor for the Liberty Tractor Company. McVicker was an established, respected name in the tractor industry. Apparently, his reputation carried enough weight to assure the government that Liberty Tractor Company was not a fly-by-night operation trying to take advantage of a sensitive situation.

So the government's charges against Liberty seem to have been dropped. However, trouble reappeared quickly, as another Liberty Tractor Company was discovered, this one in Dubuque, Iowa.

Farm Implements and Tractors said in a 1920 issue that confusion has resulted from the adoption of the same corporate name by another company but steps were being taken to overcome this difficulty. Again, the mists of time make it unclear what those steps were, as both companies existed simultaneously for a couple of years.

With all the troubles regarding tractor companies, those who would make tractors began to do more research. The P. J. Downes Company had eight years of experience with the tractor industry when it began with Liberty. According to a 1918 article in *Farm Implements and Tractors*, P. J. Downes studied the indus-

Norman Pross of Luverne, North Dakota, owns this 15-30 Liberty, a rare tractor indeed. Liberty company said this tractor represented "freedom from tractor troubles." The light-weight Liberty weighed 5,775 pounds yet easily pulled four 14-inch stubble bottoms, the company claimed. It had a 5-inch bore and 6 1/2-inch stroke with two forward speeds, 2 1/2 and 4 1/2 miles per hour. The fine adjustment of bearings allowed the tractor to be pushed back and forth on the demonstration floor with a single finger.

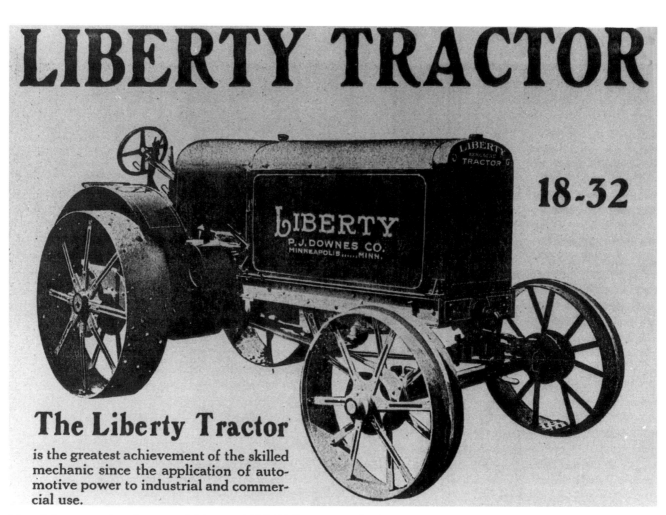

LIBERTY TRACTOR

18-32

The Liberty Tractor

is the greatest achievement of the skilled mechanic since the application of automotive power to industrial and commercial use.

Liberty's larger entry into the tractor field was its 18-32. P.J. Downes was the distribution arm for the company, and when they went into bankruptcy in 1921, that essentially also doomed Liberty Tractor Company, because business had slowed down substantially due to the farm depression.

try carefully and determined that a four-plow tractor was the most economical for the farmer because one farmer could handle four plows easily without increasing labor demands.

With this information in mind, the Liberty Tractor was designed as a lightweight four-plow tractor. It was difficult, it appears, to interest farmers in tractors without some kind of attention-getting gimmick. Pioneer Tractor Company set a silver dollar on edge on its running tractor to show how smoothly it ran; and Liberty Tractor Company claimed that the fine adjustment of bearings made the Liberty Tractor so light in draft that it could be pushed back and forth on the sample floor with one finger, which didn't, however, seem to help it in the field. Later advertising modified that to pushing it with one hand.

The Liberty Tractor seemed to be much more than gimmicks. It was a tractor ahead of its time in looks; a quick glance at the form of the Liberty Tractor

shows that it is far more streamlined than most tractors of the time.

The tractor performed well for such a light machine. When Elmer Pitcher was preparing to go to the North Dakota Tractor Demonstration in Minot, he called on Mr. Jenkins, manager of the Minneapolis branch of the Oliver Chilled Plow Works, to furnish a four-bottom plow. Mr. Jenkins scoffed at the idea of a 5,800-pound tractor pulling four breaker bottoms. Pitcher said he would show Jenkins that such a light tractor could do the job.

Jenkins was not the only doubter. At Minot, a farmer offered to bet $1,000 that the Liberty Tractor couldn't pull four 14-inch breaker plows. Luckily for the farmer, no one took up his bet. The Liberty pulled them steadily and easily. Liberty also made an excellent showing at the Fourth National Tractor Demonstration at Salinas, Kansas, where it pulled four 14-inch stubble plows for six days under all kinds of conditions without stopping once.

Shortly thereafter, at the Northern Illinois Tractor Meet in September 1919, Liberty set a record with a fuel-labor cost of 93.8 cents per acre.

Unfortunately, the distributor, P.J. Downes Company, went into bankruptcy in 1921, dealing a huge blow to the Liberty Tractor Company just as it was coming into its own. Combined with the slowing economy and increasing competition of the early 1920s, the loss of its distributor was enough to put an end to the Liberty Tractor.

Downes returned to the tractor business a couple of years later, and tried to jump-start the Liberty Tractor enterprise, but it was too late. One more orphan tractor was added to the rolls. It remains unclear how many Liberty tractors were finally manufactured and sold, but the total was probably less than a thousand.

LION

If you believed the claims about tractors in newspapers and magazine advertising in the early part of the twentieth century, every tractor ever made was one of the best, the most beloved by the farmer, the most powerful worker in the field, the most popular, and the cheapest one to boot.

So began the saga of the Lion Tractor Company of Minneapolis, Minnesota. The Lion Tractor, "strong as a lion, made of steel, sensation of the world, never tired, never hungry, never sick," was first brought into the market in late 1914.

It immediately caused an uproar, because the Bull Tractor Company claimed the Lion Tractor was actually one that they had paid D.M. Hartsough (a well-known tractor designer of the time) to create and design them. Hartsough had designed the earlier Bull Tractor, as well as the "Big 4" Tractor.

The complaint alleged that the Bull Tractor Company employed Mr. Hartsough in January 1913 to manufacture a tractor that would be better than the Bull tractor they were presently making. Hartsough allegedly accepted the commission and made a tractor that could be sold for $50 less than the price of the Bull tractor. The price difference was significant enough to spur sales, as the farmers of the time often bought simply the cheapest model. Hartsough then allegedly sold the device to the Lion Tractor Company instead of the Bull Company.

The Lion Tractor Company obtained a patent and the new machine placed on the market as the Lion tractor. The suit said the Lion name was selected in order to mislead purchasers into believing the Lion was a sold by P.J. Lyons, a well-known stockholder in the Bull

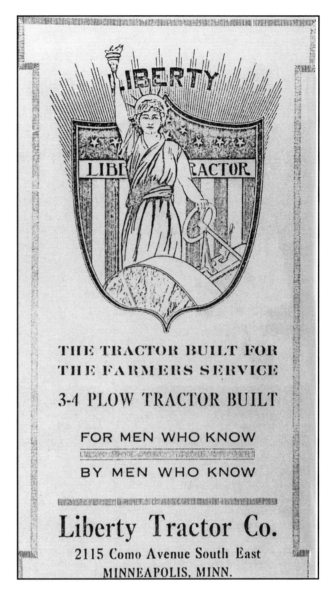

THE TRACTOR BUILT FOR THE FARMERS SERVICE

3-4 PLOW TRACTOR BUILT

FOR MEN WHO KNOW

BY MEN WHO KNOW

Liberty Tractor Co.
2115 Como Avenue South East
MINNEAPOLIS, MINN.

Liberty Tractor Company was challenged by the Vigilance Board on whether they had chosen the liberty logo and the name "Liberty" because it would give the impression it had something to do with the U.S. Government, which was already manufacturing Liberty trucks. But it appeared Liberty Tractor Company was on the up and up.

Tractor Company. A restraining order was asked, prohibiting the manufacture or sale of the new tractor by the defendant (Lion) company.

Diamond Iron Works of Minneapolis had agreed to make 5,000 of the Lion tractors, and that financing was undertaken by the Federal Securities Company (see Ford Tractor Company for more information on this company). The price was set at $345 per tractor.

In February of 1915, the courts agreed with at least some of Bull's claims. Lion Tractor Company was prohibited from making Lion tractors. Additionally, the

The only Lion tractor model ever made claimed itself as a two-plow tractor that could pull three plows and a drag and still have extra power left over. A dynamometer test in 1915 claimed 2,500 pounds pull on the drawbar. The big claim to fame of the Lion—other than the accusation that it had originally been designed as Bull Company's next tractor and was sold illegally to Lion—was that all the weight was above the two wheels of the tractor so no power was lost to pushing dead weight ahead of it, as it claimed other tractors did. The 8-16 tractor sold for $475 in 1915.

court discovered that the Lion Tractor Company had very little material on hand, and that only three had been put on the market, and a fourth was being built. Bull said they were continuing to make both the Little Bull and Big Bull to the limit of their manufacturing capacity.

Officials of Lion Company claimed they weren't affected by the injunction that said they weren't supposed to make any more Lion tractors, because the particular Lion tractor the injunction talked about was of a tractor they had never manufactured and did not intend to manufacture. The Lion tractor, said the officials (of Lion), was in no way affected by the injunction in question.

Even though Lion Tractor Company had been told to stop making Lion tractors, they decided they were not going to take this injunction without a roar. They simply ignored it. Against the wishes of the court, and of course Bull, they continued making Lion Tractors.

The great claim to fame of the Lion Tractor over other tractors was that it was the only two-wheel tractor manufactured. It was so constructed that its entire weight was directly on the two great drive wheels. In all other tractors a third to one-half the weight was carried on the front wheels, requiring power to drive this dead load over the ground. In the Lion Tractor all of the pow-

er was utilized, for a large gain in power and proportionate saving in fuel, the claim was made. Magazines said the popularity of the Lion Tractor continued to increase.

On May 15, 1915, the courts struck again: they fined Lion $300 for contempt of court for not obeying the injunction that said they couldn't continue to make tractors that embodied a distinguishing feature of the traction engine designed and invented by D. M. Hartsough, a differential brake steering device identical to the differential brake steering device embodied on the machine designed and invented by D. M. Hartsough.

Lion appealed, but meanwhile, they changed the construction of the differential brake steering device.

At the end of 1915, the company was reorganized, with new officers, and a change of name, adding "Inc." By now the price of the Lion was $475, still attractive to small farmers. Because it was light it could travel safely over poorly constructed bridges where heavy tractors would not dare venture. The lightness also meant it could travel in wet soil and light soil much better than the heavier machines.

Another advertisement listed everything the Lion Tractor had been used for: on separators as large as 28 inches, as well as for plowing, harrowing, discing and hauling, grinding, shelling, cutting ensilage, sawing, hauling road graders, and more. The ads bragged, "Tell us what the LION hasn't done."

As the court controversy raged, *Farm Implements* wrote Lion and asked for their side of the story. Lion answered: "So much misleading information has been disseminated by various public reports referring to this case that a statement appears largely useless." Lion said even though Bull claimed they owned the machine Hartsough had invented, Hartsough claimed independent proprietorship. "The machine was tried out," Lion says, "by the Lion Company and abandoned as worthless. The Lion Company never manufactured the machine or sold it and the case from the outset, from our standpoint, has been a matter of practically moot consideration."

The company goes on to say that the machine they were selling was designed and patents gotten from "wholly independent parties" than Hartsough, and that the old order was not in power any more with Lion.

"Misleading public statements have been spread," Lion said, "broadcast to the effect that the case to which reference is made above, involved patent rights, which was not fact. It has also been sought in various ways to make it appear that the machine there in controversy was the same which the Lion Company has been manufacturing and selling."

About a year later, *Farm Implements* said in a headline, "Lion Tractor Company settles patent litigation." They also said "The Lion has been in the field for two years and has proved satisfactory in all sections of the country."

Well, maybe not; two years after that, for unclear reasons—most likely competition and farm recession, Lion, which made certainly fewer than a hundred tractors, folded, and its tractor became another orphan.

LITTLE GIANT

When Mayer Brothers Company of Mankato, Minnesota, began touting its Little Giant tractor, based on 40 years (one newspaper report said 25 years) of service in the manufacturing business (also machinery repair business), nobody knew what bitter feelings would result.

Louis and Lorenz Mayer began in Mankato in 1876 with a machine shop that eventually was named Mayer Brothers, Inc. They built gasoline and steam engines and fixing machinery. In the early years of the twentieth century, they began experimenting with tractors.

In 1911 they built the first Little Giant tractor. One of their advertisements said, "We know of no way we can make our tractor better."

Under a headline in their advertising "What the Little Giant Tractor Will Do For You," was the typical list of what the Little Giant would do on the farm. But the last line was curious: "Yes, and it will make farming so interesting that your boys will rather remain on the farm than leave for the city."

Mayer Brothers was not afraid to take a gamble. After noting the possibilities in the agriculture field, they hopped full-force into the tractor-building field in 1914 and discarded the work they had been doing for nearly 40 years. Four former Mayer Brothers employees banded together and started the Enterprise Machinery Company, which was essentially the old Mayer Bros. Inc. Enterprise Machinery intended to go into the machinery repair business, and manufactured tractors, trip hammers, and road graders.

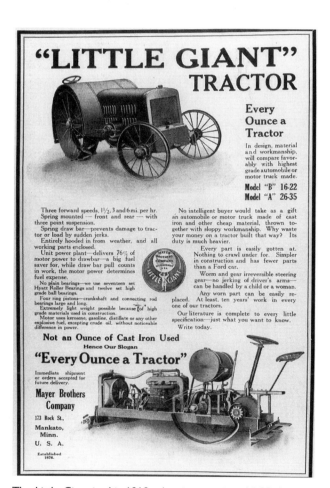

The Little Giant in this 1918 advertisement is a 16-22. Later it was downgraded to 12-22, and was called a Model A. The Mayer Brothers got involved with building tractors, but then either lost interest, or were somehow ousted from the company, which was renamed Little Giant Company. The Model A had speeds of 1 1/2, 3, and 6 miles per hour. The Little Giant-built engine ran at 900 rpm. The Little Giant Model A had a 25-gallon fuel tank with a 5-gallon reserve, weighed 5,200 pounds, and sold for $1,250 in early 1915.

Mayer Brothers offered a large and clear warranty in its advertising of The Little Giant Tractor: "The seller warrants the Little Giant Tractor to be made of good material and workmanship, and when properly adjusted and operated, to develop its full horsepower rating on belt and drawbar.

"If any parts prove defective in material or workmanship within one year from date of shipment from factory, and such parts are returned transportation charges prepaid to the seller at Mankato, Minnesota, new parts in place thereof will be furnished by the seller without charge, f.o.b. Mankato, Minnesota."

Also, Mayer Brothers enlarged their factory in 1917, until they had three times the floor space of the old factory. The company had asked for more capital at an annual meeting of stockholders, and the wish was granted. The company was apparently doing well, because the money for the improvements came from the profits.

O.M. Hatcher, manager of the company, said Little Giant was securing a large volume of export trade, which he expected to increase rapidly with the close of World War I. The plant wanted to increase from 110 to 150 workers if the men could be found.

So all in all, the business was strong, monied, and growing. One of the early advertisements pointed out one of the pressing needs on the farm: hired help. "Every farmer…operating a farm of 80 acres or more, can solve the hired help problem with the Little Giant oil tractor." In 1915, a 22-16 and 35-25 were both built.

In 1918, the name of the plant was changed to the Little Giant Company. In a cryptic line, *Farm Implements and Tractors* on December 31, 1918, says "The change was made principally because the Mayer Brothers are no longer interested in the company." The impression is given that the Mayer Brothers got out of the business. Perhaps they had an inkling of what was coming.

On May 27, 1919, workers asked for higher wages. They were acting on encouragement from the War Labor Board, which recommended wages for first class machinists, 72 cents per hour; second class, 65 cents per hour; specialists and handy men 56 cents; and helpers, 40 cents. This was based on an eight-hour day. Mankato was the only city in the district that was not paying the standard scale that the War Labor Board had recommended. Actual wages were 30-40 cents an hour.

Workers asked for the increase in the morning, and were told the plant couldn't afford the increase. At 11 A.M., the workers, who also wanted the recognition of their union, were locked out. The newspaper contin-ued, "owing to the attitude the company has taken toward the demand for more wages the men have decided not to go back to work until they get what they have asked for in the raise in wages as well as the recognition of the Union by the company and an eight-hour day." Work days were 10 hours at the time.

The company's reaction was swift. They placed a wild and inflammatory advertisement in Twin City papers (Minneapolis and St. Paul): "WANTED—Non-union molders, blacksmiths, and machinists of all grades; good wages; 60 hours weekly excepting three summer months are 55; not a minute lost time during last 41 months; business growing fast; ground door opportunity for good men; living reasonably cheap; splendid churches and schools, including state normal and parochial institutions; union locked out here; we are running steadily, but short handed; we want men who will stick and grow with us—red-blooded Americans, not the IWW's Bolsheviks and the like. Little Giant Company, Mankato." The IWW—Industrial Workers of the World—was an international industrial labor union organized in Chicago in 1905, and sometimes used questionable methods. It disintegrated after about 1920.

An article in *Minneapolis Labor Review*, talking about how manager O.M. Hatcher would not meet with anyone who did not work in the plant, was just as vitriolic and scandalous: "Those choice stool pigeon herders and spy gatherers, K—— and G——, of Minneapolis, have invaded Mankato. The one strike breaker he was able to inveigle into his services is now repining in the Mankato Bastille, and will remain there for the next sixty days as the result of his conviction on the charge of carrying concealed weapons….The picket lines are strong at Mankato. The workers are standing in solid array, and the Little Giant Company commences to look like even a bigger boob than the advertisement would indicate it to be."

Despite the inciting headlines of the newspapers: "Little Giant Company, Enemy of Bolsheviks and Justice, Locks Men Out" and "Red Blooded Americans Asked To Become Slaves," somehow the sides began to find common ground. State mediators were called in during August 1919, and the lock-out was settled. Little Giant Tractors—which had a solid reputation in the tractor field—continued to be made and sold, almost unchanged for the next eight years.

The Little Giant tractor was never a major player in terms of numbers sold, and it became an orphan tractor. Despite this, its parent company survived and continued to build power hammers among other products.

Chapter Five

Megow *to* Minneapolis Threshing

MEGOW CONVERTIBLE

If every article or advertisement about tractors printed from about 1910 to 1920 could be believed, the world would today be swimming in tractors like the Klumb, Espe, and Me-Go. Especially the Me-Go.

In 1917, a rumor persisted that Henry Ford had considered making a tractor using his automobile motor as a power generator in a small tractor. The Convertible Tractor or Megow (or Me-Go) was just such a machine.

The rumor was quelled, perhaps because Ford introduced a tractor of his own, the Fordson.

Rumor also had it that Henry Ford himself said that in a few years the tractor industry would outstrip the automobile industry.

ME-GO CONVERTIBLE TRACTOR ATTACHMENT

DEALERS WRITE FOR ATTRACTIVE PROPOSITION

CONVERTIBLE TRACTOR CORP.

The drive-wheel of the Megow Convertible Tractor had steel lugs and could be attached to a usually-Ford car in about an hour to use in farm work. A special water-cooling system also had to be installed, and was guaranteed not to overheat the vehicle at any speed. No single pinion carried the total load, and the power distributed equally through the entire system of enmeshed gears, so no single parts wore out through overwork, the company claimed. Orders came in from South Africa, Australia, and England, and for a while prospects looked good.

Charles F. Megow, one of the leading experimental mechanical engineers of the Ford Motor Company, took matters into his own hands. He dreamt up the Convertible Tractor, a conversion kit for the Ford car into a tractor. Megow, E.J. Megow, R. E. Gehan, E. W. Helms, and J. B. Van Vechten formed the Convertible Tractor Corporation.

Charles F. Megow had strong tractor industry credentials: he worked with Bucyrus Company, was chief machinist of the Asiatic squadron of the U. S. Navy for five years, designed trucks, joined the Marmon Automobile Company, then the Maxwell Motor Company, and his work was so prominent that it attracted the attention of the Ford Motor Company. In solving the low-priced tractor prob-

This is one of many advertisers who flooded the market around 1920 to convert a car—usually a Ford—into a tractor. The possibility must have been heady—to convert a car into a farm tractor for $325 and an hour's worth of work. Several dozen companies sold these kits, as Megow did in this one (also called the Me-Go), but the concept didn't last long. It was just too much trouble to change back and forth, not to mention the dirt and damage problems from driving in a field all day.

lem, Megow used the automobile as the base.

In 1920, a wide variety of tractors appeared that weren't strictly tractors. All kinds of wacky machines, which were combinations of cars, trucks, and tractors, were produced.

The advertising for the "Me-Go" Tractor says "The 'Me-Go' Tractor Attachment converts a Ford Car into the most efficient Farm Tractor ever offered. We guarantee 1,000 pounds of drawbar pull."

The concept was simple. In less than an hour, a farmer could change a Ford pleasure car into a practical farm tractor with a few simple tools. Changing it back to a car required only half of an hour. It wasn't even necessary to remove the fenders on the Ford, or alter the car in any manner, except to remove rear wheels and adjust the water connection when attaching the Dual system on the motor. The Me-Go was guaranteed not to overheat the engine, and attached to the Ford, could pull two 14-inch plows and do all the farm work of four to six horses.

Megow offered a money-back guarantee on a 10-day trial as positive evidence of the manufacturer's faith in the product and a forceful selling argument for the dealer.

Originally, the Convertible, or Me-Go, tractor, was to be set together in the Convertible Tractor Company's factory in St. Paul, Minnesota, bringing the parts in from several subcontractors. In 1917, with World War I raging, iron and steel products became difficult to get, so Megow bought his own factory to create the parts he needed. The factory was located at 1485 Marshall Avenue in St. Paul.

His thinking ran thus: with 7,000,000 small farms in the United States, all of whom would need at least one tractor, surely he could sell 3,000,000 of those farmers on the cheap ($325) Convertible Tractor. That meant building 30,000 tractors a year for 100 years. He used that logic to get himself dealers, advertising that the cost of making the machine was $65, and the machine would be sold to farmers for $250 (later changed), and the dealer would get a 25 percent commission, or $62.50 per tractor. He totaled up the amount of profit to be made on all the tractors, and the millions sounded just great. He had dealers in Upper Midwest, and claimed to have sold tractors to all corners of the United States, as well as Cuba.

His thinking was also an answer to the farmers' cry for a simple, cheap tractor that anyone who was capable of operating an automobile could run. Megow thought he had it with the Me-Go Convertible Tractor.

The tractor was thoroughly tested. In the spring of 1916, Megow bought a cast-off car for $35, and used his kit to convert it into a tractor. The resultant Megow Convertible Tractor was used on Minnesota farms throughout the season in doing all kinds of farm work, from pulling a gang plow through quackgrass to hauling a self-binding harvesting machine.

Results were so good that farmers who saw it at work were loud in their praise and profuse with orders for the tractor attachment.

A Minnesota farmer, C. R. Cleland, recommended the Megow: "The Megow Tractor is not like the ordinary tractor which can be used only a few weeks during the year, but in my opinion, the Megow Tractor can be adapted to so many uses that it is an article any farmer can use on his farm every day in the year."

Right
Charles F. Megow had strong tractor industry credentials when he developed the Me-Go Convertible tractor attachment. Some of the Me-Go advertisements pushed the envelope ("Tractor for $250), but the company was a flash in the pan so nothing was done about the ads. His "tractor" appeared at a time when farmers were wishing for multiple-use vehicles, because they hadn't been proved impractical yet.

ME-GO CONVERTIBLE TRACTOR ATTACHMENT

utilizes power at two opposite sides of wheel—one pushes, the other pulls, thus equalizing the strain. With this distribution of applied power there is no one point that performs all the work. No single pinion carries the total load. The power is distributed equally thru our entire system of en-meshed gears, and no single parts are wearing out thru overwork.

See Our Exhibit and Demonstrations at Minnesota State Fair.

Price $250 F. O. B. Twin Cities.

State and local distributors wanted.

CONVERTIBLE TRACTOR CORP.

1485-1487-1489 Marshall Ave.   ST. PAUL, MINN.

Megow Convertible products were made in a large two-story factory 60 x 115 feet long at 1485-7-9 Marshall Avenue in St. Paul. Each convertible unit was thoroughly tested before it was shipped from the plant. Megow figured there were six million farms of less than a thousand acres, and 4.3 million of 20 to 174 acres, and those were the farms that would be most interested in the Megow Convertible Tractor add-on. He knew farmers had been clamoring for a small, light-weight tractor for these farms, and he figured he'd struck on the way to provide it for them. Unfortunately, the company only lasted a few years after its 1917 inception, and didn't sell nearly the 3 million he figured he might.

The attachment could be made to any car, from a Ford to the most expensive touring car. It fit them all. Megow figured the concept would be a hit, because he figured small farmers couldn't afford both a car, which was becoming very popular, and a tractor. So why not, in a sense, get both? "With the Megow Convertible Tractor," the newspaper says, "the farmer can plow with his car, sow with it, till with it, harvest with it, haul with it; and he can use it to run stationary farm machinery—do almost anything with it. Then they can use it for pleasure—take the family to church, to town, to the picnic, with it." No mention is made of what to do with the dust and dirt that might fill the interior.

Megow also suggested that when a car was worn out for pleasure driving, it could be turned into a worker on the farm, or a worn-out pleasure car could be purchased cheaply and made do the field work of six or eight horses.

Megow reported that one of his dealers wanted 10,000 of the Convertible Tractors the first year, providing shipments could be made April 1, which Megow said would be impossible, so he wouldn't be able to honor that contract.

He continued with his pie-in-the-sky assessments: that he would have a workforce of 500, that they could produce 100 tractors a day, that the factory would work for 312 days a year (31,200 tractors a year)—and on and on.

Early advertising indicates that Megow may have built a tractor (rather than just a kit) at one point. One of their early flyers refers to C. F. Megow as the, "Inventor of the Megow Convertible Tractor and of the Megow Tractor." If such a tractor was ever developed and sold, there don't appear to be any of them around.

Unfortunately, Megow, like many other of the "combination tractor" people, misread the market. They figured that farmers, pining for the feel of reins in their hands, dreaming of days gone by, wanted not pure tractors, but tractors that could get down and dirty but also serve all other purposes for the family, like going to town.

But it didn't work out. Megow's Me-Go Convertible Tractor never worked out, and the company and its tractors and attachments became orphans.

MINNEAPOLIS STEEL AND MACHINERY COMPANY (TWIN CITY TRACTOR)

Minneapolis Steel and Machinery Company was an innovator. One of its early models, the Twin City 40, had power steering. The company's large engines all cranked from the operator's platform. They also made narrow tractors to prevent side draft, and Minneapolis Steel and Machinery Company (MSMC) was the first to build a four-cylinder, sixteen-valve engine, the TC 12-20. The company also published a regular bulletin to keep workers apprised of what was going on in different departments, held tractor schools to teach farmers how to work their machines, and more.

The Weekly Northwestern Miller, a Minneapolis publication, gives great insight into what plants were like at this time. In an April 1903 issue, the publication describes the MSMC factory, "All the buildings are of brick and steel construction, and aside from being very substantial, are made practically fire proof. ...The three main shops, which are built in accordance with the most advanced ideas, are each provided with an electric traveling crane of 25 tons capacity, traveling the entire length of the building and spanning a space of 60 feet. By the use of these cranes, both heavy and small pieces of machinery can be picked up and quickly carried to any-place desired. ...Compressed air is used in the operation of riveters, chippers, hoists, etc. Crude oil is employed as fuel for the furnaces. All the shops are heated by steam, and are lighted by electricity produced by the company's

This older model Twin City 40-65, from about 1913, has a short cab top, unlike later models with longer tops. This picture was taken on the main street of Martin, North Dakota, pulling a 10-bottom plow. One of the advertising ploys for the 40-65 was the statement that you couldn't deny that the tractor looked good, and it was just as good as it looked. Twin City 40s claimed the largest crankshaft, bearings, and strongest frames and steel gears of any tractors on the market.

Notice the longer canopy in this later Twin City 40 tractor. By this time, the tractor had incorporated power steering, and was one of the company's most popular tractors. It weighed almost 26,000 pounds, and sold for $5,000. It was paired with Bull tractors (along with several other Twin City models) in advertisements in *Gas Review* in 1915, at a time when Minneapolis Steel & Machinery was also making the ill-fated, but popular, Bull tractors.

The Twin City 40-65 was redesigned and brought to market in 1911 by Minneapolis Steel & Machinery Company. Note the short canopy on this photo. An article in the *Modern Gas Tractor* in 1922 discussed how to stop a tractor, most specifically a Twin City 40: "The first step is to close the throttle, throw out the clutch, retard the spark lever, and apply the foot brake. If the stop is to be a lengthy one, the engine may be put out of operation by throwing off the ignition switch and closing the gasoline valve at the tank. The clutch lever should always be kept in the 'off' position unless the reverse lever is provided with a 'neutral' notch, in which position it is not connected to either forward or reverse drive gears and then the master clutch may be let in if desired." Just as lengthy information was given for starting the tractors.

own plant. The company has on its premises over a mile of railroad tracks, and a switch engine of its own to handle cars on these tracks."

For the first few years MSMC built steam engines, bridges, gas engines, and in 1910, hired another company, the Joy-Willson Company of Minneapolis, to build a tractor for them. This was done in 1910-12, and results were so encouraging the Twin City Tractor was born.

MSMC built tractors for other companies while building its own Twin City tractors. The company built Case 30-60s for J. I. Case. They had a million-dollar contract with the Bull Tractor Company to build Bull tractors.

In 1914, MSMC contracted with a Canadian co-op to build the Twentieth Century Tractor. This tractor was quite similar to the Bull Tractor, which was upsetting to Bull. The Bull Company persuaded MSMC to refuse to sell the Twentieth Century Tractor in the United States for one year. Shortly thereafter, MSMC stopped making Bull tractors, saying they were forced to neglect their own tractors if they made Bulls.

Farm Implements discussed "Why A Tractor Should Be Built Narrow" in a February 29, 1916, article about the

Many of the Twin City tractors were not only powerful tractors and efficient, but were also beautifully styled, like this Twin City 17-28. Originally it was a 12-20 model, but after further testing was re-designated 17-28.

Twin City tractors: "Side draft has always been an element in the operation of small tractors that manufacturers have found it difficult to eliminate in the construction of the machine….When a tractor…is only capable of pulling from four to six plows, if it is built wide, as a machine must be when its motor is placed crosswise on the frame, side draft is bound to develop, especially if the machine is to be kept upon hard ground. In the small sizes of the Twin City tractors, this difficulty has been eliminated by building unusually narrow machines. The Twin City 15 brings out this point in a very clear way. The machine will pull four plows under ordinary conditions, the width of which is practically the same as the width of the machine, which is about five feet. This enables this little machine…to pull its full load of plows without any side draft whatever. …The Twin City 15 has a vertical four-cylinder motor and is built almost identically the same design as all the larger sizes of Twin City tractors."

Though it's not clear when the Twin City Tractor School was started, a January 1915 advertisement says

Cutting grain with a binder, this Twin City 17-28 was dwarfed by the crop in the picture about 1930. This was one of the tractors that was incorporated into the Minneapolis Moline line after Minneapolis Steel merged with Minneapolis Moline Plow Company in 1929. A large farm owner in West Australia bought one Twin City in 1926, and liked it so well that he bought seven in all, including three 17-28s. These were the kinds of farmer testimonials that kept Twin City tractors in the forefront.

The 27-44 was built by Minneapolis Steel and was almost identical in looks to its smaller cousin, the 17-28. The size of Twin City tractors was always plainly marked. Twin City logos were undoubtedly one of the most beautiful logos on the tractor market, as well.

Twin City built a 25-45 tractor for seven years, until 1920. By the time they were building this tractor, Twin City had given up making Bull tractors and the Twentieth Century Tractor, which they built for a Canadian co-op, and were concentrating on their own. Additionally, they sold engines to a number of the well-known tractors from that era, including Reeves, Hackney, and Sawyer-Massey.

Five about 1919 Twin City 12-20s are either plowing on a big farmer's farm, or being demonstrated. Clay County in Minnesota bought 12-20s new in 1919 for maintaining roads in the county. Just a year or so after this picture was taken, the price of new 12-20s was reduced to $1,395, an aftermath of the deepening farm depression. It was the lowest price in the history of the tractor, the company claimed. The 12-20 was powered by a four-cylinder engine.

"Read What Former Students Have Done": "I had no experience around engines of any kind," wrote Earl McFadden of Neche, North Dakota, on November 14, 1913. "Facts speak loud, thus the following: I started with a Twin City 40 and during the summer and fall months I cut 900 acres with four binders, broke 145 acres of timothy sod, plowed 1,000 acres besides several days threshing. During this entire time I had little or no trouble. Having had no previous experience, I lay my success, and justly, to the valuable training secured at the Twin City Tractor School. I cannot speak too highly of this school, and I gladly recommend it to any and all young men."

MSMC advised taking a vacation in Minneapolis, and finding out how these tractors ran. One of the teachers at the school, C.E. Bramhall, said, "As I travel from place to place, in hotels, and on the streets of small towns, I catch a familiar phrase—'Twin City Tractor.' That sounds good to my ears, for nobody but the field

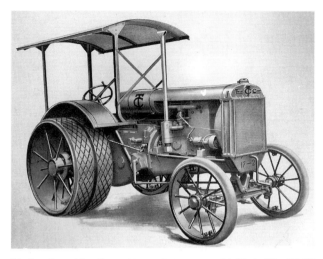

Notice the rubber front tires and canopy on this Twin City 17-28 from the late 1920s, not too long before Minneapolis Steel and Minneapolis Moline merged.

The 16-30 Twin City from about 1916, this tractor was compared to the streamlined looks of automobiles, although the speeds certainly couldn't be compared. It only went 2 3/4 miles per hour. Doubtless this was one of the tractors that was used to teach in the Tractor School that Minneapolis Steel put on at the time. Many farmers who took the courses were highly pleased with them. H. W. Adams conducted classes at the school, as he had for his earlier Common Sense Tractor School, and was hired in 1918 by the Minneapolis School Board to provide the first tractor classes given anywhere in U.S. public schools.

These North Dakota farmers are cutting grain with a binder about 1930 using a Twin City 17-28. North Dakota farmers had kind words to say about Twin City tractors, and many were used there.

The logo of a Twin City 60-90, the largest of the Twin City line. It carried almost 100 gallons of fuel, weighed 28,000 pounds, was almost 22 feet long and as high as wide, about 10 feet. This was one of the tractors that was used during instruction at the Tractor School classes.

A Twin City 12-20. This model was loaded onto the back of Twin City truck about 1919, and driven overland from Minneapolis to Wichita, Kansas, not only to give farmers and dealers close-up looks at the 12-20, but also to determine how good the Twin City truck was. At the time, the factory had built two experimental models of 3 1/2-ton Twin City trucks, and had them running, while a pair of experimental two-ton trucks were being built.

The Twin City "40-65"

A Twin City 40-65. These behemoths were in the Minneapolis Steel catalogs from 1911 until 1924, and were the first of their line to contain power steering. Earl McFadden, a North Dakota farmer, wrote that he'd used a Twin City 40 and during the summer and fall months cut 900 acres with four binders, broke 145 acres of timothy sod, plowed 1,000 acres besides several days threshing. During this time he had little or no trouble.

expert knows how hard it was to convince the farmer in the early stage of the game that he had a real tractor. But in those days we did not have schools to teach the farmer and his son how to operate and care for a gas tractor….It appears to be a common fault with our field experts to be jealous of their tractor knowledge, for they do not instruct the owner or operator as to the proper care and up-keep of his tractor." That made for more work for the field expert, no doubt.

About 1917, the payroll for MSMC was the largest of any manufacturing company in the country. In the July 1919 issue of *Bulletin*, MSMC's employee magazine, the reader gets a real sense of the camaraderie within the company: "If we keep on growing, the drafting force will soon be recognized as a real department. We now number 19, against 6 last December.

"For a time, Buffington's trip (around Lake Superior in a car) was in doubt, due to the fact that someone decided to appropriate his Buick (right out of the garage) and tried to sell it to a farmer in St. Paul. The only trouble was that the farmer turned out to be a detective.

"Our best wishes go with Newell for he was a very constant worker during his stay with us. Now Pete won't have any one to pay for his lunches."

Additionally, *Bulletin* says, "This department (Automotive Engineering Department) has turned out a variety of new 'jobs' recently, and for the benefit of those who don't know, we list them below:

"TC 12-20 Tractor (now in production)

"TC 20-35 Tractor (now being built)

"TC 3 1/2 Ton Truck (two experimental models built and running)

Minneapolis Steel and Machinery Company advertised heavily in the farm magazines of the time. It wasn't unusual for them to run full-page ads month after month, which was a testament to their success.

"TC 2-Ton Truck (first two experimental trucks being built)

"TC 12-20 Crawler Tractor (design and detailing practically complete)."

Another page discussed the trip a new Twin City 12-20 tractor took from Minneapolis to Wichita. A picture was taken on the day of departure, near Rosemount, Minnesota. The purpose of this overland trip from Minneapolis to the Wichita branch was a dual one—to give farmers and dealers in the territory covered an opportunity of making a close examination of the "12-20" and also to test out the new Twin City Truck.

Meanwhile, MSMC continued to crank out tractors. In 1929, Australia's largest wheat grower used Twin City Tractors. P.W.G. Liebe of Wubin, West Australia, said he purchased his first Twin City in January 1926, and it worked so satisfactorily that he had since made further purchases, all of which gave entire satisfaction, until he had seven Twin Cities in all, four 27-44s and three 17-28s. He considered the Twin City the best wheel tractor on the market, and hundreds of satisfied buyers agreed with him.

So if it was so great, why aren't Twin City tractors being made today? Simple. In 1929, MSMC merged with the Minneapolis Moline Plow Company to form Minneapolis Moline Power Implement Company, and the Twin City Tractor was dead.

MINNESOTA THRESHER

One little-known orphan tractor company that had a curious history was the Minnesota Thresher Company of Stillwater, Minnesota. For one, the company helped

Front view of a late 1870s Minnesota Thresher Company engine, called the "Stillwater Boiler." Made to burn wood and coal, it had a large direct flue and small return flue, which gave it more heating area than a direct flue of larger surface. It was perhaps a surprise that the company ended up making and/or selling any at all, with as much time as they spent in court with at least three suits they launched, and a fourth against them. In 1889 their main production was threshers, of which they made four a day, along with two of the engines, with 350 workers.

prove a Minnesota law unconstitutional, and seemed to spend more time in court than it did building farm equipment. For another, they used prison labor to manufacture their products.

The Minnesota Thresher Manufacturing Company was organized to succeed the Northwestern Car Company in the late 1880s. The Minnesota Thresher Manufacturing Company (MTM) went to court very shortly thereafter. Thomas Lowry and R. B. Langdon were the owners of stock in the old company to the tune of $25,000 each. They declared half a dozen 2-percent dividends to themselves and a couple of other choice stockholders at a time when the Northwestern Car Company was being operated at a loss. MTM wanted to get that dividend money back, and to do that, brought suit against Lowry and Langdon to recover from each the $3,000, which it was claimed had been wrongfully paid out as dividends.

The loss was considerable—$3 million dollars for the Northwestern Car Company, which Minnesota Thresher was still indebted to pay. So it didn't make sense to Minnesota Thresher that some of the principal stockholders of the old company should be getting dividends when everyone else was losing money.

By some means or other, Langdon and Lowry, who owned or pretended to own a large amount of the stock of the concern, were paid regular 2 percent dividends on their stock out of the profits of a concern that lost $3,500,000. MTM claimed the money that went to these men should instead go to them.

Meanwhile, Minnesota Thresher was involved in another lawsuit, this one against them. Two men had

This is a side view of the Stillwater Boiler, which the company claimed was so safe because of the arch of the boiler that no reports of accidents had occurred from the many hundreds of boilers that were out working. The oval figure to the left is a cross-view of the boiler. Sediment would settle naturally into the ash pit, the company claimed.

tried to get the forfeiture of the charter and franchises of MTM. The Minnesota Supreme Court, however, decided the reason the suit had been brought was merely to prevent Minnesota Threshing from collecting claims that were made against stockholders (the first suit mentioned above) because of the fiasco of the Northwestern Car Company.

Then there was a third suit. In this one, Minnesota Thresher tried to collect money from two other defendants who got dividends from Northwestern. "The works and accounts," wrote *Farm Implements and Hardware* in October 1889, "were purchased from the receiver by the Minnesota Thresher Manufacturing company, which now attempts to recover the money (which had been) paid out in dividends."

There was a fourth lawsuit, as well. In a newspaper article dated January 2 in Boston, it said, "The suit of Theodore Converse, receiver of the Minnesota Thresher Manufacturing company against John B. Myers of this

The Stillwater Traction Engine was another of Minnesota Thresher Manufacturing Company's products. The company took over the debt of Northwest Car Company (making railroad cars), and spent much time in court trying to get some of the poorly-spent money back. Two of the principal owners of Northwest Car had given themselves dividends, while the company had been losing more than $3,000,000.

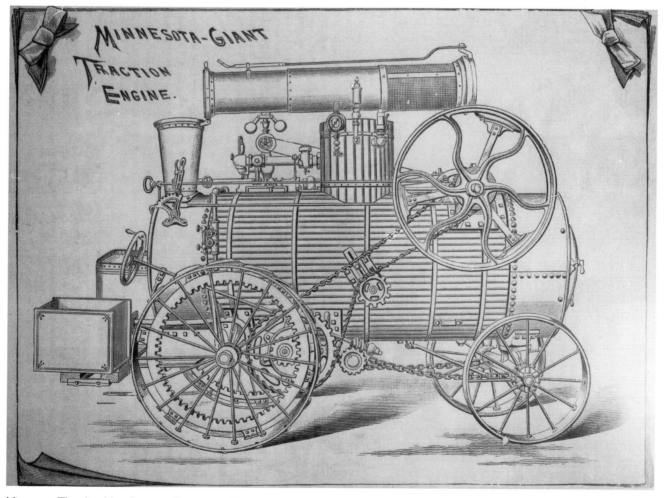

Minnesota Thresher Manufacturing Company of Stillwater, Minnesota, was best known for its "Minnesota Giant" traction engine. The company used prison laborers from the Minnesota State Prison, located in Stillwater, for a couple of years, although they dropped the method as ultimately unsuccessful.

A top view of the Stillwater Traction Engine, another Minnesota Thresher Manufacturing Company product. Figures 2 and 3 show the application of power to traction by the traction clutch and also by the reverse clutch.

defendant, for the reason that it tended to enlarge his liability as a stockholder. He was a stockholder before the law was passed, and the law was, therefore, retroactive.

"The corporation was capitalized for $7,000,000, and its failure was a large one." Perhaps because of all the adverse publicity, a number of stockholders didn't cotton to the leaders of Minnesota Thresher Company, and when the stockholders meeting was held in February 1890, according to FIH, "The meeting was followed by the publication in the *Pioneer Press* of the statement that a movement was on foot to put the company into liquidation. This statement has been vigorously denied by the officers who state further that the present management is acceptable to all except a small minority of the stockholders, and that at this meeting the unissued stock was subscribed for and the business shown to be in an exceedingly prosperous condition. ...The *Pioneer Press* report is credited to a disgruntled stockholder."

Minnesota Thresher used convicts from the prison in Stillwater, but that work didn't seem to be a success. *Farm Implements and Hardware* said, "The labor of the convicts (of the prison at Stillwater) has not been

city, to enforce the liability of a stockholder for the debts of the corporation, under a law passed in Minnesota in 1899, was decided by Judge Fox of the Superior court.

"The court found for the defendant (Converse), holding the law of Minnesota unconstitutional as to the

The development of steam traction engines took a heavy toll on roads and bridges. This Minneapolis machine tumbled into a creek in North Dakota. The bridges of the day just weren't built to carry such heavy loads. *Richard Birklid Collection*

an unmixed blessing to the Company and as the contract of the Company with the state expires September 1 we may expect to see the next season one of far greater activity outside the walls of the prison than this last one has been inside those same walls. The Company will utilize several large buildings for machine shops that have heretofore been used for storage."

Sometime in the middle of all of this, MTM kept building a variety of equipment, including a steam traction engine, "The Minnesota Giant," although only a few of them. It's unclear when the company became defunct, and its steam traction engines became orphans.

MINNEAPOLIS THRESHING

John MacDonald figured he'd move on to bigger and better things than owning the MacDonald Manufacturing Company in Fond du Lac, Wisconsin, so he packed up his company and moved to Hopkins, Minnesota, in 1887.

Not much remained of the Hopkins, Minnesota's Minneapolis Threshing Machine Company plant after a tornado ravaged it in 1925. The buildings in the background were demolished. Perhaps this huge loss led to its eventual merger to become Minneapolis Moline. *Richard Birklid Collection*

This photo of a rare return-flue Minneapolis steam simple engine was taken near Nome, North Dakota, in 1911. The engineer is Oscar Huseby. None of these machines are found in working order today. They could burn coal or wood, but nothing else without a special adapter. *Richard Birklid Collection*

The Minneapolis 35-70 tractor threshing in this photo was originally rated for 40 horsepower. The tractor didn't quite make 40 in its Nebraska Tractor Test in 1920, and the rating dropped down to 35 horsepower. A farmer near Comstock, Minnesota, owned three of these, and used them to plow night and day until his five sections of land were finished. The belts connecting the tractor with the separator were 150 feet long, and though they looked dangerous and unwieldy, few threshers were ever injured by them. *Richard Birklid Collection*

These thresher people took a break from their hard work in 1913 to get a picture taken of the new Minneapolis 40-80 gas tractor. The tractor was teamed with a 40-inch threshing machine, as indicated by the divider board and two men pitching on each side. Old-timers said four men—two on each side—were needed for pitching when a 40-inch threshing machine was used. The machine was almost 12 feet high, 23 feet long, and 10 1/2 feet wide. Wheels are 7 feet 4 inches high and 30 inches wide. The radiator held 110 gallons of water and had 342 half-inch tubes, each three feet long. *Richard Birklid Collection*

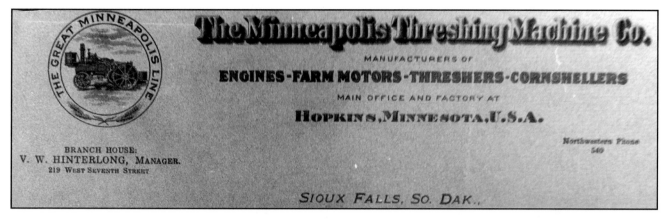

Stationery from the Minneapolis Threshing Machine Company office in Sioux Falls, South Dakota, in the early 1920s. The Minneapolis Threshing Machine Company was one of the companies that Philip Rose visited in his quest to find a solid company for General Motors to buy to get into the tractor business opposing Henry Ford. *Richard Birklid Collection*

At first he produced threshers, including the Pride of the West and the Victory threshers, with the slogan "We can make you money. We can save you money." When the Victory was granted the only medal awarded for a complete steam outfit at the World's Columbian Exposition in 1893, the name was changed to the Columbian Victory Separator.

MacDonald saw the advantage of producing steam traction engines, and the Minneapolis Threshing Machine Company soon began selling tractors out of the Huber Line from Marion, Ohio. In 1889 MacDonald began selling his own steam traction engines.

All looked good for the newly-named Minneapolis Threshing Machine Company, which employed six hundred during the busy season in 1897.

But looks can be deceiving. MacDonald had saved himself from financial ruin once in Fond du Lac, and it appeared he was a man who liked to take chances. In 1897, he wanted to build gasoline engine tractors, but couldn't convince his company to do so.

In *Farm Students' Review* for May 1897, the writer lauded Minneapolis Threshing Machine Company, and at the same time chastised other manufacturing companies: "It would do some of our easygoing brothers good to visit this institution and take a lesson or two from them in the ways of economizing time and labor. Where a machine can be used to save manual labor or save time such a machine is obtained at once. Every man in the employ of the company works at some special part of the machine year in and year out. In this way he becomes expert in his line of work and gains speed and skill the longer he works. It would be a very difficult and costly task to have one man make a whole machine himself, but when each man works at his own special part of the machine it results in faster and more accurate workmanship."

Unfortunately, MacDonald was bounced out of his own company in 1899, before he could produce his much-desired gasoline tractor.

The man who took over, Minneapolis banker Fred Kenaston, had a different view for the company. He bought a Toronto company (John A. Abell Engine and Machinery Works), which entered him into the huge Canadian market, and then bought Advance Thresher from Battle Creek, Michigan, and combined the three companies into American Abell Engine and Thresher Company. He made a profit by selling Abell to Rumely in 1911.

A Minneapolis 25-50 cross-motor engine stacked with people in this 1912 photo, probably built by Northwest Thresher Company of Stillwater, Minnesota, whom Minneapolis Threshing Machine Company had contracted to build the tractor for the first couple of years of its existence, until the Minneapolis Threshing Machine Company could build it themselves. It was a short-lived tractor, going out of existence in 1914. It contained a four-cylinder vertical motor with jump-start ignition. *Richard Birklid Collection*

About the same time, the Minnesota Threshing Machine Company ran into some problems with the Minnesota Commissioner of Labor. In a return letter, the President and Treasurer Kenaston wrote that he'd been notified that fans and suction pipes were needed to be installed in the tumbling room adjacent to the foundry, "for the purpose of taking away the dust and making better ventilation. We wish to advise you that just at the present time it will not be convenient for us to make these changes, for the reason that we are in the midst of our season's work and it would involve the stopping of a portion of the work which we need and the laying off of several of our employees while these changes were being made. We wish to assure you, however, that just as soon as we close down our factory at the end of our season's run, on September 1st, it is our purpose to make a number of changes and additions to our factory, among which will be the proper ventilating of and dusty carrying appliances in the grinding and tumbling room. In as much as the present tumbling room has been in use for a number of years, we imagine that two or three months further use of it will not be a serious matter to your department." No record exists of the results, although one must assume that the government very seldom loses.

America had about 28 million horsepower in animal and mechanical power on farms in 1910. Mechanical power (almost entirely steam) represented approximately 6 1/2 million horsepower, or 24 percent of the total. So the market was there, and every tractor company knew it.

In 1911, the Minnesota Threshing Machine Company added Universal gas tractors to their existing steam tractor line. The Universals were made by Universal Tractor Company of Stillwater, Minnesota. They also contracted Walter McVicker, pioneer of several tractors, to design an original tractor for them; Northwest Thresher Company in Stillwater contracted to make 25 of these Minneapolis Farm Tractors for the Minnesota Threshing Machine Company. Several other models

By the time this ad was published, the Minneapolis Threshing Machine Company had branch houses in most of the Midwest states and in Saskatchewan. They also had representatives in Texas, Louisiana, and New Mexico, where they were represented by the Southern Minneapolis Farm Power Company of Dallas.

In this ad, the Minneapolis Threshing Machine Company talks about how farmers should not necessarily buy the cheapest tractor, but rather the best power machinery they could get.

were built in the next few years, but none were as successful as the steamers had been. A 1919 advertising folder issued by the company discussed their separators, as well as the 15-30 tractor.

The company was one of the well-run ones that Philip Rose visited in 1915 for the purpose of finding a tractor company that General Motors could buy, and swoop right into the tractor market. Rose wrote, "Mr. Kenaston never makes a move until he sees where he is going to land. He had made money in the threshing machine business when others have lost because he never loses his head. Besides this business is not his principal activity." In a sense, this showed even more what a genius Kenaston was.

In 1929, the tractors of Minneapolis Threshing Machine Company became orphan tractors as the company was merged along with the Minneapolis Steel and Machinery and Moline Plow Company to form the Minneapolis Moline Power Implement Company.

A double-cylinder Minneapolis engine of 35 horse pulling disk plows, loading up on coal and water, about 1910. The double-cylinder engine was generally made in one casting. The double cylinders were one-piece cast, parallel, and bolted to the boiler. *State Historical Society of North Dakota*

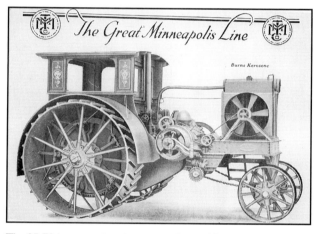

The 35-70 kerosene-burning tractor from a Minneapolis Threshing Machine Company catalog was equipped with a valve-in-head four-cylinder motor. The catalog made a special point to mention the fact that the gears had covers. The 35-70 was a popular tractor in the Minneapolis Threshing Machine Company line. It had been downgraded from a 40-80 due to Nebraska tests, and stayed in the line when the company merged and became Minneapolis Moline in 1929.

This Minneapolis simple steam engine came in 20, 24, and 28-horsepower sizes, and the boiler was a full-water bottom type, which the company claimed was the favorite of thresher operators. It was more expensive to build than the open-bottom type boiler. It was safer and gave more room for mud and sediment below the fire line. This butt-strap steam boiler could also be lawfully operated in any state.

Chapter Six

Pan *to* Russell

P~AN~

The Pan Motor Company's farm tractor generated lots of press and promotion, but never really amounted to anything. Samuel Connor Pandolfo had a strong life insurance business, selling 100 million dollars of it to the scattered farmer-rancher population in Texas, Oklahoma, Arizona, and New Mexico, in the first decade of the twentieth century. Out on the road as much as he was, cars became a passion of his (he owned 37 of them) and when the insurance business went into a turndown, he decided to build a better car. He was a visionary man, and he thought for a long time before he decided. He considered a wide range of areas and cities throughout the United States, many of them offering inducements to bring his company there, until he finally narrowed it to Minnesota. He wanted a place that would supply as

A photo of the only Pan Tank-Tread Tractor ever built, sitting outside the Pan Factory in St. Cloud. It didn't run, even though area newspapers had proclaimed how disappointed farmers had been at the National Tractor show at Kansas City in 1918 when the tractor came late. The papers also claimed that hundreds of farmers who had already left for home turned around to come back and view the tractor, and that many more were disappointed that they couldn't get their Pan Tank-Tread Tractor immediately.

many needs as possible for his new business. He figured that city was St. Cloud, Minnesota, and he began there in 1917.

From the beginning, he was a wheeler-dealer; he sold $10,000,000 in stock, built a factory, five dozen houses, a hotel, and was planning a hospital and school. The factory consisted of 14 buildings, all connected by underground tunnels. His car factory actually got off the ground and produced the Pan Car. The tractor operation wasn't quite as successful.

During all the hullabaloo, Pandolfo also came up with the idea to build a tractor. Advertisements screamed, "Pan 'War Tank' That Will Win The War. Now is the time when man power must be conserved. The Pan Tank-Tread Tractor saves man power and takes the place of eight horses."

Pandolfo knew how to play on patriotism. His ad said, "Thousands of our young men have gone to

You know the kind of a car you want everybody wants. We are confident that we know, too. *It's the* PAN.

Pan cars were the first products produced by Pan Motor Company of St. Cloud, Minnesota. Cars were a passion of Samuel Connor Pandolfo's—he owned 37 of them when he was selling insurance to scattered farmers and ranchers in the Southwest. Because he did so much driving, his thoughts led to building a better car, and once he was into that, he decided to make a tractor or two as well.

war, to make the world safe for democracy. It is now up to us to do our part at home. We must raise bigger and better crops. We must do our work with less help and in less time. The Pan Tank-Tread Tractor will do your work better and in less time at a saving of one man and eight horses."

One of the big features of the Pan Tank-Tread Tractor was the adjustable control. With that special equipment a farmer could steer the Pan Tractor from a seat on the plows, binder, or any other machinery the tractor was pulling. This made steering the Pan Tank-Tread Tractor just as easy as driving a team of horses.

The *St. Cloud Times* of February 27, 1918, says "Without a question the Pan Tank-Tread Tractor proved the biggest sensation at the National Tractor show (at Kansas City) from the moment it went in to action until the closing hour of the show." It was also shown in the lobby of a hotel in Des Moines. The paper went on to say that other tractor men could not conceal their surprise and admiration when they inspected the "Farmer's War Tank." "Hundreds of farmers," the paper said, "who had visited the show at

WILL REMIND YOU THAT
THERE'S MONEY IN PAN FOR YOU

The logo of the Pan Motor Company was used to urge dealers to take on the product. Many people said the Pan car was actually a very good product, so the Pan tractors may have been decent, as well. But Pandolfo, the inventor, never made enough money to carry through, and was eventually indicted for fraud.

Kansas City the first three days—before the Pan tractor arrived—came back to see the Pan. That it made a decidedly favorable impression was evident by their remarks. Many showed their disappointment when they found they could not have a 'Tank- Tread' delivered at once. ...There is no tractor just like it. Some say it is revolutionary. It is revolutionary—it will revolutionize the tractor industry—it will revolutionize farming, in the opinion of many."

Other magazines took up the refrain, claiming the Pan Tank-Tread Tractor was solving a vital issue especially for the wet regions of Northern Minnesota where large tractors weren't able to travel. It was the latest addition to the tractor world built along the lines of the famous war tanks, yet could be operated by one man, and would do for the farmer what hardly any other machine can do.

In 1919, Pan Motor Company held a parade in St. Cloud for the tractor. The *St. Cloud Daily Journal* wrote on October 9, 1919, "The parade was guided through the city by the 'king of the field', the big Pan tractor. This was followed by the big Pan trailer bus carrying the band members. The bus was drawn by the tank tread tractor, the 'tractor that isn't', as stated by one of the directors of the firm." (This is the first mention that the tractor actually worked—which is perhaps not odd, considering that most articles about tractors or any machinery for that manner don't say, 'and yes, the tractor ran.')

Curious that the director would put it that way; from the start, it appears the Pan Tractor was, if not a hoax, not on solid ground. The wheels had started to come off the Pan Motor Company machine, so to speak.

A suit had been filed against Pandolfo in Chicago, claiming the Tank-Tread Tractor was not only impractical but was a physical impossibility. But the St. Cloud papers said the Pan, the best caterpillar tractor so far designed and developed, had run under its own power, ap-

The logo for the tank-tread tractor was similar to Pan's logo for his car company. One of the special features of the Pan Tank-Tread Tractor was that the farmer could steer the tractor while sitting on the seat of a binder, plow, or any other machinery the tractor might be pulling. Pan also made tractor fenders for early Fordson tractors.

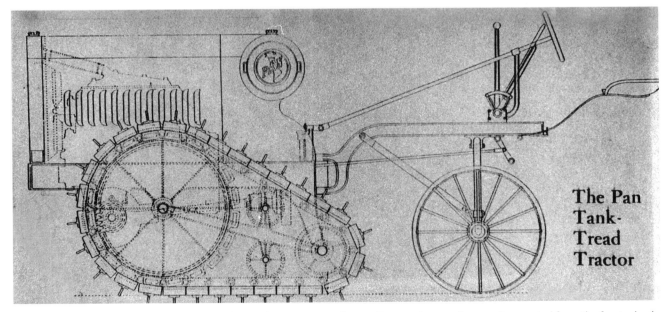

The Pan Tank-Tread Tractor

These are schematics of the Pan Tank-Tread Tractor. It was an unusual caterpillar-tread tractor because it operated from the front wheels. Claims were made that that was so it could more easily be used on wet and sandy soil. Since the machine never ran except for a very short while, there was no way to prove—or disprove—the extravagant claims made for it. One claim that was disproved was Pan's claim that the Tank-Tread Tractor would win World War I.

The second tractor Pan designed and wanted built was called the "King of the Field," and was to go along with one of his Pan automobiles, which he called the "Queen of the Road." Very little is known about this tractor. One way Pandolfo got positive advertising for his company was to pay a publisher of a magazine an extra $450 to put out extra copies of two different magazines, each of which was highly complimentary about Pan Motor Company. The tractor was priced at $1,750 and was to have been made for $850.

peared on the streets of St. Cloud on its own power, and was a success. It had been severely criticized because of its front-wheel drive, which was a radical departure from the accepted configuration for this type of tractor. However, that criticism was only because people didn't understand the true purpose of the tractor, which was to be used on sandy and wet soil and ground that is soft.

Despite the positive spin on things, more bad news was to come. In a pamphlet by the National Vigilance Committee (which monitored advertising) dedicated to the Pan Company, the company's bubble was burst: only one model of the much promoted Pan Powered Tank-Tread Tractor had been built, and instead of by Pan, by the Progressive Machine and Model Works, 119 Southeast 5th Street, Minneapolis.

The pamphlet goes on to say the information given out at the Kansas City show was certainly optimistic, since the tractor was not in running order at the time, but was there merely for show. There was never any surge of farmers coming back to view the tractor because it was such a wonderful product.

Pan had plans for a second type of tractor, as well, the "King of the Field," as previously mentioned. There is very little information available on this tractor, although there are illustrations of it.

Pan Motor Company was involved in the tractor business in another area; it made fenders for Fordson tractors. After the Pandolfo Motor Company went bust about 1920, leaving 70,000 investors in the lurch to the tune of $10,000,000, Pandolfo himself went almost non-stop into court, where he was finally indicted and sentenced to 10 years in prison for a variety of frauds in different areas of endeavor besides Pan Motor Company. The truth appears to be that he was an extremely likable man who probably believed everything he said he could do. In the end run, however, he couldn't, as he'd promised, build a tractor that would revolutionize farming. He could only create another orphan tractor.

PIONEER

Perhaps the saga of the Pioneer Tractor Manufacturing Company of Minneapolis and Winona, Minnesota, is not really a mystery.

Perhaps logical explanations exist for why a company that once operated in buildings of several hundred thousand square feet; made the best tractor of its time; projected a work force of more than 500; manufactured tractors big as elephants; sold them worldwide; and invented the modern-day war tank would not get mentioned in the centennial history of Winona, numerous county histories, or the obituary of its Winona president.

Begun in Minneapolis in 1909 or 1910, the company first manufactured the Pioneer field-motor and auto grain separator. Within a year, the company was removed to Winona. E. M. Wheelock and C. F. Loomis

went with to Winona to continue in the active management of the business. The stock in the company was owned by a number of Winona businessmen, together with the Minneapolis stockholders.

Winona was excited about their new business. A headline in the *Winona Daily Republican-Herald* of Saturday, February 19, 1910, screamed, "Gas Traction Engines." "This industry is the manufacture of gas traction

Left
The Setran brothers from rural Douglas, North Dakota, were en route from their farm, hauling five wagons full of wheat to Douglas elevators about 1915, using their Pioneer 30-60. This stylish tractor had a glassed-in cab (as did the larger Pioneer 45), and even had a rear curtain. The drive wheels were 8 1/4 feet high, and the monster could cut a 32-foot swath of grain at one time, but its cooling system required only 27 gallons of coolant. One farmer who bought a Pioneer 30 in 1910 dropped in at the factory after one year of use, and ordered a second one, saying he was going to sell 33 of the 35 horses he used on the farm, and he figured it would save him $3,600 in his farming of his 1,600 acres the next year. Pioneer urged farmers to come to the Pioneer factory in Winona, Minnesota, to see how the 30-60 was made. In 1911, the company still called them "traction engines." One farmer kidded that when the Pioneer's engine misfired, you saved a quart of gasoline. *Richard Birklid Collection*

The Pioneer 18-36 was the smallest Pioneer tractor. Brown and Company was a distributor of Pioneer tractors in Fargo and Bismarck, North Dakota, and ordered sales cards for their representatives to take out to give to prospective buyers. This was one side of one of those cards; on the reverse was a stamp advertising Brown and Company, the representative, and Pioneer. *Richard Birklid Collection*

engines, the coming machine which is already being used to quite an extent in farm work and in time will very largely take the place of horses."

It was said first shipments would be made in April, and would average one per week, June 1 two per week, and after July 1, the factory would produce one per day. Railroad car shipments from Minneapolis were arriving daily and several cars of steel from the roller mills were in transit.

A. C. Johnson, general agent of the Chicago and Northwestern Railway Company, predicted that the gas engines built by the Pioneer Tractor Manufacturing Company in Winona would easily take a leading place in the tractor field. His conversations with experts in South Dakota said those machines made in Winona had decided advantages over anything else in this line so far put upon the market.

A huge demand was beginning to develop for gas engines used in breaking land, plowing, seeding, harvesting, threshing, and even marketing, as one engine had power sufficient to haul several loaded wagons. There was

every reason to believe that the location of this industry to Winona would be one of the most important business events that had occurred for Winona for a long time.

One engine was turned out a week, but after July 1910, one a day was planned, enough work for 500 employees the next summer. Pioneer had more orders than could be filled in 90 days.

The building leased was a two-story brick building, 140x95 feet, while the frame building adjoining it, the erecting and arranging shop, was 160x35 feet. The workforce consisted of 25 people, with E.M. Wheelock as manager of the works.

Two styles of tractor engines of four sizes were manufactured, a 40-horsepower, 25-, 15-, and 8-horsepower machine.

A year later, a supplement to the *Republican-Herald* said this was normally the dull season in the tractor line, nevertheless this Winona enterprise was working a night as well as a day crew continuously. It had already outgrown its original home. Now its machine shops occupied the entire former floor space of

Western Minnesota Steam Threshers owns this rare Pioneer 30-60 and displays it yearly at its September reunion near Rollag, Minnesota. The 30-60 was a powerful beast used to break sod in North Dakota and Texas, and for heavy pulling jobs. Pioneer also claimed to invent the war tank, and considering the size of some of the machines they built, it's plausible.

A stylized drawing of a Pioneer 18-36. Though it was a smallish tractor for Pioneer, it still weighed 6,000 pounds and was recommended for four 14-inch plows and a 28-inch thresher. The Pioneer Tractor Company disappeared, and curiously enough, its existence was never acknowledged in the obituary of one of the founders, nor did his grandson know about his involvement in the company.

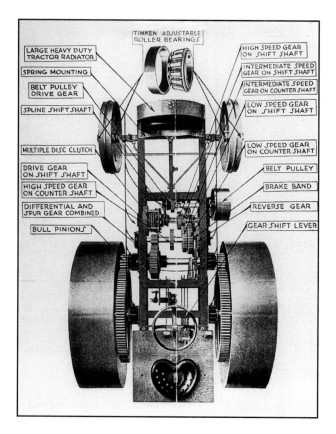

LARGE HEAVY DUTY TRACTOR RADIATOR

SPRING MOUNTING

BELT PULLEY DRIVE GEAR

SPLINE SHIFT SHAFT

MULTIPLE DISC CLUTCH

DRIVE GEAR ON SHIFT SHAFT

HIGH SPEED GEAR ON COUNTER SHAFT

DIFFERENTIAL AND SPUR GEAR COMBINED

BULL PINIONS

TIMKEN ADJUSTABLE ROLLER BEARINGS

HIGH SPEED GEAR ON SHIFT SHAFT

INTERMEDIATE SPEED GEAR ON SHIFT SHAFT

INTERMEDIATE SPEED GEAR ON COUNTER SHAFT

LOW SPEED GEAR ON SHIFT SHAFT

LOW SPEED GEAR ON COUNTER SHAFT

BELT PULLEY

BRAKE BAND

REVERSE GEAR

GEAR SHIFT LEVER

the whole establishment and its erecting department occupied an added space of 35x300 feet; its wheel and frame department 36x115 feet; its pattern, carpenter, paint, and tin department 35x150 feet; offices 40x50 feet. A big business.

The Pioneer tractors were suitable to plow the large tracts of ground in North Dakota wheat fields and heavy wax lands of Texas, and their claims at this point seemed substantiated.

More than a year later, they crowed that their predictions of success had been proved true. "In early spring the company expects to be on the market with a replica of the Pioneer 30 with a rating of 15 to 20 horsepower, for farms unsuited to the brutish 30s." By this time the Pioneer 30 had proved itself as an all-purpose

Left
This exploded overhead view of a Pioneer tractor showed the advantages of the different parts of Pioneer tractors. In *Modern Gas Tractor* in 1922, Pioneer control group levers were discussed, including the regulation of motor speed by the usual spark and throttle levers forward of the steering wheel, three hand levers, one of which was reverse, operating on a notched segment for neutral, forward or reverse, and the clutch. The magazine article also commented on the comfort of the upholstered seat and the completely enclosed cab.

tractor, and also as a road-making engine, especially in the southeastern United States.

Tractors had been placed throughout the western United States as well as in Canada and Mexico. Pioneer claimed they were trying to achieve perfection in making the Pioneer 30 and were definitely making a better machine so far as material and workmanship were concerned than most of the automobiles on the market. The owners were reportedly enthusiastic about their machines.

About 1916, Pioneer built experimental tractors with a six-cylinder horizontally opposed engine of the same bore and stroke as the 30-60. These tractors were rated 45-90, and had rear wheels nine feet tall. They did not go into production.

In December of 1918, the *Winona Independent* wrote that Pioneer was sending two dozen large machines to Russia for farm use. Machines were also sent to Romania, Austria, and Hungary.

The Pioneer 30 won a first, second, and third in three different foreign-government contests. In Romania, Pioneer tractors won gold over 11 other engines. In Russia, at the 'Kief trials,' the Pioneer 30 won second, and 9 of a possible 10 points of merit. The operator won five figures in cash. One agent said that if Europe enjoyed normal conditions the next year, they would require about 150 of the tractors.

Pioneer also may have invented the war tank, not so odd a proposition when one considers that their tractors weighed in at 11.5 tons. In 1914, Pioneer's E. M. Wheelock came up with the idea of a bullet-proof, self-propelled conveyance. The basic outline that Wheelock proposed was very similar to the early tanks (although he is not given credit for developing the tank). His design had caterpillar treads, a gas engine propelling it 10-15 miles per hour, armor protecting the operators, but the frame made of pipes for easier shipment as well a smaller target, and when destroyed, replaceable with other screw-in pipes. Wheelock tried to sell the idea, but the United States, Canada, and Britain turned it down. Two years later, the *Minneapolis Journal* reported that funny-looking cheese-boxes were going over the top and chasing the Germans. A study revealed that the equipment was exact in design to the plans and blueprints submitted by Wheelock.

From this point on, Pioneer went downhill. In 1924, the business name was changed to Pioneer Tractors, Inc., an implement business. Minnesota state records say it was incorporated in 1910 and its charter ran out in 1925.

What killed Pioneer? Perhaps a suit over its warranty, which was perhaps the best in the business— probably too good; but nobody, including a grandchild of its Winona president knows for sure; in fact, the grandchild didn't even know C. M. Youmans had ever run a tractor company.

The Pioneer 15-30 Special in this 1918 advertisement was a three-speed kerosene tractor with a four-cylinder, four-cycle horizontally opposed engine with a 5 1/2 inch bore and a 6-inch stroke.

And when C.M. Youmans died on November 24, 1946, his long obituary mentioned varied activities of his long life—but nary a word about Pioneer.

In the end, Pioneer was orphaned by one of its own parents. The company became another example of tractor companies that thrived for a short time and then died.

RUMELY

Perhaps it is true that what goes around comes around. For after a long life, during which Rumely bought out and orphaned a host of tractor companies, their company met the same fate at the hands of Allis-Chalmers Company.

The Rumely Company began, in a sense, with a pistol-whipping in Germany in about 1840. Young Meinrad Rumely, who was in the military, as his son William N. Rumely wrote later, "made the mistake of stepping forward a few inches beyond the line of the company. The captain observing the mistake, rushed toward him and struck him a severe blow with his pistol. Rumely fainted and fell, and was taken to the military hospital where he suffered great pain for several days. ...Upon being dismissed from the hospital, Rumely

The Rumely Company developed its own magazine for Rumely employees. The magazine included plant happenings and a wide variety of other information to keep Rumely employees informed as to what was going on in the plant. New lightweight Rumely Oil-Pulls had been introduced at the time this copy of the magazine came out, but the new tractors weren't enough to keep the Rumely Company afloat.

went to his home and told his parents of the brutal treatment he had received. He decided then to come to America, and his parents provided him with sufficient money for the trip." Otherwise it was likely that Rumely would have stayed in Germany as a member of the military, for he was already in military school.

Germany's loss was America's gain. Meinrad Rumely came to the United States in 1848 (where all his money was stolen from his trunk in New York), and eventually walked to Canton, Ohio, where his brother John was employed as a pattern maker for Russell and Company—another eventual orphan tractor company—of Massillon, Ohio. Meinrad did a variety of work, making pumps, erecting threshing machines, getting his first acquaintance with the type of machine that later was to make his name known throughout the civilized world.

He worked as a machinist, and eventually made his way to LaPorte, Indiana, because the railroad would be locating shops there. He made fast friends with John Faller, who urged him to start a machine shop and foundry and locate there at once.

For the next 20 years the Rumely Foundry made castings for railroad car wheels, locomotive cylinders, drive wheels, and more. In 1854, the Rumely Brothers

Right
This advertisement announces different model Rumelys, including the L (15-25), M (20-35), and S (30-60). Rumely tractors were successful for a long time, partly because of the different models of tractors they made. But the progress of other tractor companies eventually caught up with, and surpassed, Rumely.

In 1910, this Rumely E 30-60 was operating in a North Dakota field. A 1912 newspaper photo shows "The World's Greatest Shipment of Oil Pull Tractors," where 100 brand-new flatcars, mostly of the 30-60s, were being shipped 1,100 miles from St. Paul to Winnipeg, pulled by one of the largest locomotives in existence. It had to be; the Model E 30-60 was a two-cylinder machine that weighed 26,800 pounds, and had a 10-inch bore and 12-inch stroke. Most of Rumely's 30-60 production was shipped to Canada.

All Gears run in oil baths
Completely enclosed job
"Ball bearing"-Three sizes

Model "L" 15-25 H. P.
Model "M" 20-35 H. P.
Model "S" 30-60 H. P.

Announcing

THE NEW LIGHT WEIGHT

OilPull

The Rumely Toehold is pulling a disk in an orchard. The Toehold was an experimental tractor, so very few of them were made. Every tractor company created different models to see how they'd work, and if there seemed to be too much rework, or if farmers and testers didn't seem enthusiastic about the product, or for a number of other reasons, these experimental tractors didn't go into production.

The Rumely Gas-Pull in this North Dakota photo is operating a thresher. Note the gas barrels to the left, which show that this is not a steam rig, which needs barrels of water, but rather a gas tractor. The Rumely Gas-Pull was a very rare tractor, with few of them made. *Richard Birklid Collection*

The tiny Rumely 8-16 was selling for $750 in 1915 while the 12-24 three-plow tractor was selling for $975. One of the new features of this 8-16 was complete control of the entire outfit from the operator's seat, and it was made for the small farmer. Several of Rumely's tractors resembled machines made by other companies, as this one resembles three-wheelers from other companies, at least one looks very much like Twin City tractors (the 35-70 Gas Pull), and a couple of other models look like smaller Twin City tractors. More than likely it is all coincidence, but some could have been built for Rumely by other companies.

Company started making threshing machines and won a silver medal for first place against four competing threshing machines. In 1881, the new Rumely thresher was perfected and proved to be a huge success.

What was probably not a huge success was the partnership between Meinrad Rumely and his brother, John. In 1882, Meinrad and John parted ways. In 1887, the M. Rumely Company was formed by brother Meinrad.

Despite the apparent family strife, the Rumely people were innovators. If they needed a machine for the factory, they made it. Each year the company used 450,000 feet of lumber; 175 tons of steel boiler plate; 500-600 tons of pig iron; 30 tons of steel castings; and 100 tons of bar iron and steel.

After several disastrous fires and explosions, the plant was rebuilt and improved. In 1890 after rebuilding, the new cupola or melting furnace was 40 feet high and 38 inches in diameter. The new building was a veritable green house containing 2,988 panes of glass, which made it more nearly a glass house than any building in the city.

Rumely made traction engines—one in 1907 was touted, "An ordinary-sized man can almost walk under the boiler without stooping." Prototypes for Rumely tractors were built in 1908, and tested very successfully in 1909, when the area newspaper wrote "...the M. Rumely Company is the first concern to manufacture and place on the market a machine which uses kerosene." It was nicknamed "Kerosene Annie," and was

the forerunner of the Rumely Oil-Pull, 100 of which rolled off the assembly line in the new plant in 1910. In 1909, Rumely Company also designed a new "trademark," as its new logo was called, showing the plant, the western hemisphere, with lines radiating from LaPorte to all the parts of the world.

Though the Oil-Pulls were highly touted, they did have some troubles. Elmer M. Ransburg, of Quincy, Michigan, a Rumely Company serviceman, says one time they tried pulling eight 16-inch plows in a pasture that

Rumely GasPull Tractor (15-30 h. p.
Easily Makes a One-Man Outfit

This 15-30 Rumely Gas-Pull from about 1912 was a change from most of Rumely's Oil-Pull machines, and proved to be much less successful. Though huge tractors were still needed to break some sod that had not yet been broken, this was a time of flux in the tractor field as companies tried to figure out what tractors farmers wanted. *Richard Birklid Collection*

This 30-60 Rumely Model E from around 1913 was one of about 57,000 Oil-Pulls of all sizes that were made by Rumely before bad debts took them out of the business in 1915. The trademark for Rumely showed lines emanating from LaPorte, Indiana, to all over the world, which symbolized Rumely's worldwide distribution.

hadn't been plowed for some time. "I reported to the factory that we were having trouble pulling the 8-16 plow. They answered saying if I could not pull those plows with the 30-60 they would have to call me in and send someone else in my place." They never did get that job done.

During the next couple of years, Rumely gobbled up a series of other companies but weakened itself financially. In 1915, the M. Rumely Company, and its subsidiary, Rumely Products Company, were foreclosed upon and sold. This seems impossible when one views records of the old tractor companies, and realizes that the Rumely Oil-Pull was one of the four or five most reliable tractors and the Rumely Company one of the most reliable in all of agriculture.

Not long after bankruptcy, Advance-Rumely Thresher Company. Though it made some progress, it was never the company M. Rumely had been.

New lightweight Oil-Pulls were introduced in 1924, which helped Rumely stay alive, but the hand-

Right
An interior view of the cab of the Rumely Gas-Pull tractor, showing the location of levers and general layout. The Gas-Pull was not a successful tractor for Rumely, and is very rarely found today.

The Rumely Do-All was a tractor touted to do just what it's name said: everything that needed to be done on the farm. Though it was not a successful tractor in the Rumely line, it was successful in that it was a forerunner of today's general purpose small farm tractor.

No Other Tractor Can Match the OilPull on the Belt

YOU can safely invite comparison of the OilPull with any tractor a prospect has in mind. You will have the advantage in belt-work comparison, as well as ability in the field. And the buyer expects belt work from his tractor these days. Consider the following features of the OilPull for any belt job. Decide for yourself whether they are salable advantages.

(1) **STEADY POWER**
due to close governing.

(2) **OIL COOLED**
no overheating—no cracked water jackets

(3) **DIRECT TRANSMISSION**
all power delivered direct to belt.

(4) **GREATER BELT CLEARANCE**
due to patented shifting front axle.

(5) **TRIPLE HEAT CONTROL**
produces cheaper, more efficient power.

(6) **POWER**
to meet any emergency.

(7) **LONG LIFE** 10-year service can be expected from the OilPull.

Where can you—or your prospects—match those qualifications for corn shredding, threshing, shelling, sawing, silo-filling or any other belt work? Even if the OilPull's drawbar ability were only equal to any other, its belt-work features alone would give you a worth-while advantage. Let us tell you what other dealers are accomplishing with the OilPull and how we co-operate with them. Write today for the facts about the

OILPULL

"ten-year service tractor"

ADVANCE-RUMELY THRESHER COMPANY INC.

(Incorporated)

The Advance-Rumely line includes kerosene tractors, steam engines, grain and rice threshers, husker-shredders, alfalfa and clover hullers, silo fillers and motor trucks

C.F. Norberg, a Rumely dealer in Hastings, North Dakota, gave out this Dealer's Card showing Oil-Pull models made by Rumely, shortly after the company had filed bankruptcy and become Advance-Rumely. Cards like this were a staple of many of the tractor companies, a way of reminding customers of the product. *Richard Birklid Collection*

writing was on the wall. It limped along until 1930, when weakened by the Great Depression, it was sold to Allis-Chalmers Company.

RUSSELL

One night in 1898, Russell and Company of Massillon, Ohio, not only stopped an opera performance, but attracted hundreds of sightseers who came 12 miles from Canton, Ohio, by bicycle, train, and carriage.

Unfortunately, the spectacle was an incredible fire, the second fire the manufacturing firm had suffered. According to the *Evening Independent* of October 24, 1953,

Left
Advertisement for Oil-Pull performance. Some of the Rumely ads played on the big word in their tractor line—"Pull," as in "After all, it's the Pull." Rumely also claimed victory over a number of competing tractors in trials at Winnipeg, but only identified the other tractors as Competitor No. 1, No. 2, etc., which lessens the impact of their claim.

"The disastrous fire (of 1898) destroyed the warehouse and killed an employee of the company. ...The Canton fire company was called one-half hour after the fire started, and arrived a speedy one hour later," which of course didn't give much hope for the survival of the wooden tractor company. The opera performance in Massillon was stopped as hundreds of persons rushed to the fire scene to find the source of the spectacular red glare in the skies. The tragedy was fitting as the era of the fire-powered steam engines was beginning to wind down.

The three oldest Russell brothers, Charles M., Nahum S., and Clement, came to Massillon in the spring of 1838 hoping to find woodworking jobs. Though they didn't get the jobs until several years later, they stayed, performing contracting jobs. Their stay in the city was plagued by fire; the first one in 1840 destroyed their wood shop; a second occurred in 1878, and the third as mentioned in 1898.

In 1842 they formed Russell and Company, for the purpose of manufacturing engines, boilers, and threshing machines. The brothers had become disenchanted with threshing machines of the time, designed their own, and in 1845 won an award at the state fair.

Soon they were selling their threshing machines abroad.

The company grew rapidly, adding more brothers until 7 of the 13 in the family were partners. Russell and Company was instrumental in getting railroads into the area to help out the overloaded Ohio Canal traffic, and ship their own plant products out.

The first major fire in 1878 put 250 men out of work, and destroyed 36 years' worth of patterns, as well as half of the plant and all the iron-working machinery. But one week later, using borrowed machinery, the iron department was in operation again on double shifts, and within 30 days the full complement of machines was being turned out again.

In 1871, the company divided. C. Russell and Company moved to Canton to make reapers and mowers. The Russell Engine Company was spun off in 1900 to make stationary engines—in 1912 that company merged with Griscom-Spencer Company of Jersey City to become the Griscom-Russell Company.

By 1909, when Russell and Company decided to go into gas-powered tractors, the plant covered 21 acres, and had produced 18,000 farm, traction, and stationary engines, as well as 22,000 threshing machines. They also made sawmills, pneumatic stackers, feeders, and steam road rollers.

The early Russell steam traction engines were prized for their simplicity and ease of repair. All moving parts were in plain sight, and any parts needing adjustments were within easy reach of ordinary tools.

Like so many of the steam traction engines, the Russells were behemoths: the smallest one they made in 1912, the eight-horsepower, weighed 9,500 pounds, and held 60 gallons of water.

They built tractors with some of the earliest cabs, which were made of wood and cost $100 extra. The cab had windows and sashes.

In 1909, Russell entered the gas tractor race, building a three-cylinder machine not of its own design, but adapted from a British tractor. Dubbed "The American," it had three 8x10 inch cylinders that developed 22 horsepower at the drawbar. Russell tractors were solidly built, like all of their products, but not particularly innovative, and that perhaps cost them part of the market share.

Russell also made other large machinery, like this huge steam shovel (The Massillon Power Shovel) and railroad boxcars. But farm-related machinery was by far the biggest staple of the company. By 1909, in their 21-acre plant, they had produced 18,000 farm, traction, and stationary engines, as well as 22,000 threshing machines.

As the composition of farms changed and needs became different, Russell went to their lightweight series of tractors. The Russell, Jr. was the first, and weighed 4,650 pounds. All gears were enclosed except for the final drive. The hooded transmission and engine gave a classy appearance.

Russell and Company, over its long history, made many other products, including train box cars and steam shovels. Russell and Company entered its final years in decline due to the rise of International Harvester, which had snatched away the market of the once-famous Russell threshing machine. The company limped on until 1942, 100 years after it had started, when its assets were sold in a sheriff's sale. Tractors were not made after 1927, although the company continued to furnish parts and service until 1942, when the Russells, another series of tractors, became orphans.

This old Russell was a return-flue type introduced in 1891, a very old self-propelled traction engine. The 13-horsepower engine used a 7 3/4x10-inch simple cylinder. The lid at the top of the stack was hinged. Note the distinctive Bull design ("The Boss") on the side of the machine.

Top left
This 30-horsepower Russell from 1908 was one of the largest Russells made at the time, and weighed 9,000 pounds, plus water. A year later, Russell decided to enter the gas-engine tractor race with the introduction of "The American," based on the design of a British tractor. *Minnesota Historical Society*

Bottom left
This 25-horsepower engine from about 1918 was called a compound. It had two pistons on the same rod, and used the same steam twice, which was supposed to make these Russells run more economically. Russell engines often had different adaptations and innovations than other steam engines of the time.

Chapter Seven

Sageng *to* Waterloo Boy

SAGENG

The Sageng Threshing Machine Company of St. Paul, Minnesota, has one of the most peculiar histories of the orphan tractor companies, and one can only wonder what might have happened if the company had been able to build enough Sageng Threshers, the major portion of its business, and the Farmer's Tractor.

This is where the short-lived Sageng Threshing Machine Company did business in St. Paul. The founder of the company, Halvor O. Sageng, was a former minister and a visionary man, but his self-propelled thresher with cast-iron gears was a bit fragile. Only 23 of the threshing machines were ever made, and none survive to this day.

Halvor O. Sageng was a minister. After graduation from Augsburg College and Seminary in Minneapolis, he was sent to Madagascar as a missionary. While there he came upon the idea for his self-propelled thresher. When he came back to the states, he organized the Sageng Thresher Company in 1908.

Twenty-three of the odd-looking threshers were built all together (none exist today), but the cast iron gears couldn't stand up to the pounding as the very heavy machine moved under its own power from farm to farm and stack to stack.

During the winter of 1909, the machine was redesigned. The *Weekly Journal* of Fergus Falls, Minneso-

ta, wrote, "The design of the machine has been materially changed, and those who saw the machine which operated so successfully this week, scarcely recognized its resemblance to the new one which they saw working last year." The trial for the threshers was done near Dalton, Minnesota, where Sageng had been raised, and where his brother Ole, an investor in the firm, lived.

He was gratified with the success of his invention. Arrangements had been made with a farmer named Fossan to keep his entire crop unthreshed until the machine was ready for its trial. It was run out from Dalton over a very hilly, and in some places soft, road and handled itself with perfect ease.

Sageng was really onto something. He made the body of the machine out of metal, which was practically unheard of at the time, to prevent fires and explosions. He had a plan for marketing the machine, wanting to get 25 of them out to different parts of the country to make sure everyone in different areas was talking about the machine; he would not take credit, but only cash.

Four sizes of the thresher were manufactured. Straw came in the back and went out the back, while the grain, which was vibrated twice as long as in other threshers to get it loose from the heads, came out the front. The majority of his stockholders were from other states—North and South Dakota, for instance—which helped give the company distant free advertising. In 1910, Sageng had enough material on hand to make 100 new threshers for the 1911 threshing season.

Sageng was ahead of his time in terms of education about the thresher. It was his intention to take prospective purchasers—thresher men and farmers' boys—into the factory during the winter months to show them how the machine was built and teach them how to use it. Also, this first output of threshers was to be sold directly to farmers so that Sageng wouldn't have to pay commissions to their salesmen—which probably gives a sense of the company's financial state. Additionally, the Sageng company kept in close touch with all the machines sent out, so that they could be kept in first-class working order.

This was contrary to what was developing in the farming industry, as fly-by-night outfits proliferated in

The Sageng "Farmer's Tractor" was an experimental engine, and though it appears at least one of them was made, it wasn't heard for very long. It was a 1911 tractor, and looked quite different from most of the tractors of that time.

This Sageng Thresher, serial No. 102, is one of about two dozen built, one of which remains at Nome, North Dakota. Halvor Sageng's brother Ole was a Minnesota State Senator at the time. The slogan of the company was "Puts hands on the plow." *Richard Birklid Collection*

The Sageng Combination Gasoline Thresher

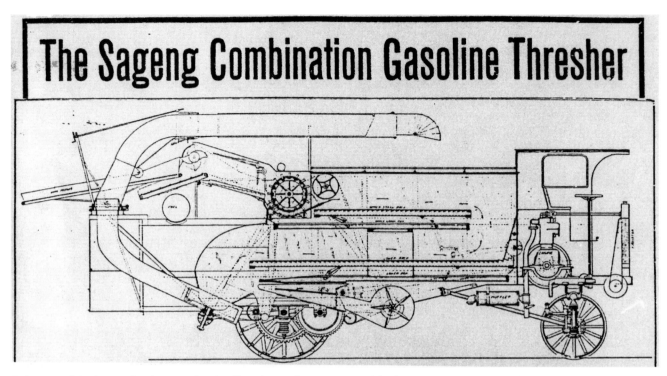

A drawing of the Sageng Combination Gasoline Thresher is all that remains of the Sageng thresher; the threshers didn't hold up in the field. The inventor, Halvor Sageng, was a minister who quit to go into the farm machinery business, but when his thresher and tractor were both unsuccessful, he went back into the ministry.

This about 1920 photo shows a Samson tractor on a GMC truck in front of the Samson Tractor Works in Stockton. A year after the purchase of Samson by Durant and General Motors, the Samson outperformed its rival, Fordson, in the Nebraska Tractor Tests. But the purchase was not a success, as Samson went down the tubes. *Rock County Historical Society*

the next six to eight years, taking money but not providing service to many farmers.

Sageng's tractor, the Farmer's Tractor, was advertised in 1911 along with the Sageng Combination Thresher. "The designing of a small tractor," the literature says, "has been a big problem to solve, and the designers of the Farmers Tractor are deserving of great credit for producing so much efficiency and common sense practicability, making it possible for owners of small farms to share in the up-to-date methods of tractor farming."

The tractor was designed particularly to meet the demand for a practical, durable, and simple farm tractor, possessing all the good qualities of the large tractor, yet adapted to the small farms at a price that owners of small farms can afford to pay.

Farmer's Tractor Sales Company advertised the Farmer's Tractor in Canadian magazines and was headquartered in Winnipeg. Unfortunately, good ideas in agricultural machinery can't work without the oil of money. Sageng and his company ran out of money, and the company went bankrupt in 1912, sending Sageng back into the ministry, leaving one more orphan company.

SAMSON

Samson Iron Works began in Stockton in 1884 to build pumps. The annual winter floods that plagued the Central Valley of California made for a fruitful market for power and pumps, and very early it stimulated the development of local industry of all kinds.

After early success, J. M. Kroyer's company had begun falling behind in the race to make engines and pumps. But the tractor business was in its infancy, a

This photo shows a young woman operating a General Motors Company (GMC) Samson on a farming operation. Samson Company won a derby of sorts; William Crapo Durant of General Motors commissioned Philip Rose to check out all the tractor companies in the United States to figure out which would be the best one for General Motors to buy (and continue a feud with Henry Ford), and Samson was chosen. This photo is from the late 1910s or early 1920s, after Samson had been bought by Durant. *Rock County Historical Society*

The Samson Sieve-Grip in this photo is from about 1918 and was taken probably at a demonstration of the tractor—notice the company men with suits, ties, and plug hats. The Sieve-Grip was a wonderful tractor for use on the spongy soil around Stockton, California, where the tractor was invented and originally intended to be used. The 12-25 Sieve-Grip was recommended for three 14-inch plows, weighed 5,500 pounds, and cost $1,350. The 6-12 Samson Sieve-Grip was recommended for two plows, weighed 4,200 pounds, and cost $775.

great market lay close at hand, and the local genius and local competition led to rapid development of Stockton as a tractor center. Kroyer's experience and developed company gave him an advantage in building tractors.

Early in 1902, the Samson Tractor existed, although the first advertising, curiously enough, seems to be in 1913. That year, the Samson Tractor won the state fair against all competition in the 6-8 horsepower category, and featured "wonderful sieve-grip wheels," which gripped far better than their open pattern would suggest. The spongy soil around Stockton led to the design, and the wheels became known as Sieve Grips because of their traction. Samson tractors were also low to create a low center of gravity for working in the hills around Stockton.

A year later, two models were offered by what had now officially become "The Samson Sieve-Grip Tractor Company." Those models were the 6-12 ($775) and the 10-25 ($1,350). The early success of the Samson was due to Kroyer, farming as a market for machinery, and

that the Samson was one of the earliest to enclose its vital parts and seal them against dirt.

About this time, William Crapo Durant, who started General Motors, was looking for a tractor company to compete with Henry Ford and the Fordson. Durant, who had built the floundering Buick Company into General Motors, was smarting over his 1908 failure to take over the Ford Company due to banking squabbles, so he kept a jealous eye on everything Ford did. He didn't want Ford to get the jump on him on anything.

Durant was an unusual person. In 1886, on the spur of the moment, Durant borrowed $2,000 from family friends and bought a buggy business after a ride had impressed him with the smoothness of the cart's suspension. The jump from horse carts to automobiles was simply a matter of time and financing. It was his spur-of-the-moment decisions that made him a wealthy man, but also lost him a fortune. Durant, according to Walter Chrysler, "could charm a bird right down out of a tree." He frequently got his way.

SAMSON

MODEL M TRACTOR $650
Platform and Fenders $50 additional
F. O. B. Janesville, Wis.

IRON HORSE $450
F. O. B. Janesville, Wis.

**MODEL "15" ¾ TON TRUCK
CHASSIS $550**

In 1920, Samson advertised three of its major products and their prices. Everything looked good, but storm clouds were looming on the horizon. In 1919, 2,888 men were employed in the Samson plant or on Samson building projects. But the agricultural depression of the 1920s as well as Durant's loss of power with General Motors ended up dooming the company.

When Ford announced plans to introduce a small tractor, Durant responded with his competitive nature and on the spur of the moment. He would build tractors as well. So he sent an independent engineer, Philip Rose, around the country to examine more than 90 companies before settling on Samson.

Durant bought the Samson Sieve-Grip Tractor Company in 1918 and looked for a manager. He spied Joseph A. Craig (eventually called "the father of General Motors in Janesville"), president of Janesville Machine Company, which built plows, cultivators, planters, harrows, and hitches.

Right
The Iron Horse was one of William Crapo Durant's ideas that didn't work out, and hastened the death of the Samson Company. Durant, who wanted to bring all the advantages of city life to the farms, figured farmers still missed holding the reins as they had for centuries in farming with animals. The Iron Horse, purchased whole and previously named the Jim Dandy Motor Cultivator, flooded the market, but was not a success because it tipped easily, and perhaps because farmers were not in a nostalgic mood for the reins of their horses.

The company had realized they needed a large investment for tractor development and a new plant. It was a tremendous load to take on, and they weren't very willing to do it by themselves.

In stepped Durant. After jockeying for position, Craig convinced Durant to move Samson to Janesville, and after buying Janesville Machine Company, he did.

Durant dreamt that he would motorize the farm, and give farmers all the advantages of other American citizens, with electricity, refrigeration, and the like. In a wise move, Durant hired experts to take care of the tractor business. Unfortunately, he couldn't keep his hands out of it.

J. H. Newmark in "My 25 Years With W. C. Durant," wrote, "We sometimes thought that the Chief never had any idea of the size of the task, nor the time required to do the job. When he would give a special task he would, in the same breath, ask when he was going to see the finished work. When called upon to do so, we would work all night, or Christmas, or New Year's. He

was hard to satisfy, difficult to please. But we loved the man—we seemed to enjoy being humiliated by him."

In 1919, 2,888 men were employed in the Samson plant or working on Samson construction projects. An 11,000-square-foot building had been completed and was producing 75 tractors a day. A foundry was 2/3 finished, and the foundation for an implement building of 517,000 square feet of floor space had been laid. Other projects were also in the works.

The future looked bright. One of Durant's first projects was reworking the Samson Sieve-Grip Tractor. The results really impressed the General Motors people, and after minor modifications, the GMC Samson tractor appeared. Unfortunately, its $1,750 list price was no competition to the Fordson, so Samson built another tractor to compete.

In fact, they used the Fordson as a model, stripping it down and making various changes that would improve it. Obviously the Samson ended up resembling the Fordson. On May 1, 1919, that new era was official-

This Model M Samson was the answer to Henry Ford's Fordson tractor. Though the standard Fordson was cheaper, the Model M came with a variety of features, which all cost extra on the Fordson. The Fordson was about 600 pounds lighter than Samson Model M. Unfortunately, Samson and General Motors lost money on their tractors, while in 1923, Henry Ford provided the world with 50 percent of its tractors. Any kind of battle that might have existed between Henry Ford and William Crapo Durant was officially over, with Ford the clear winner.

ly ushered in. Samson Tractor Company began to produce ten units a day of the Model "M" Samson tractor.

A year later, Samson outperformed its rival Fordson in Nebraska Tractor Tests. But the Samson cost more, and GM was losing money on it. Meanwhile, Samson designed the Model A tractor, but it was never produced.

Durant bought the manufacturing rights to the Jim Dandy Motor Cultivator. Immediate plans were made to flood the market with the Iron Horse (as it was renamed). Durant figured most farmers missed working behind horses, holding reins in their hands. So he envisioned a Samson tractor with reins, gasoline powered, and called the Iron Horse.

They had hoped to realize excellent profits from the Iron Horse, because motor cultivators were very popular at the time. But lack of capital, customer resistance to a poor product (it tipped easily, among other problems), and the Depression forced a hasty abandonment of the Iron Horse.

This extravaganza did not set well with the new financial backers of General Motors, the DuPonts. The venture probably confirmed the earlier fears of the DuPonts that Durant took long chances, that he did not safeguard stockholders' money, and that he was hasty in his judgments. In 1920, Durant resigned. If this had all been a battle between him and Henry Ford, Ford had won, as indicated by the 100,000 Fordsons made in 1923, half of the world's production.

In addition to tractors, Samson built other vehicles, including Samson whole-family car (a nine-passenger touring model built in 1920 and designed to take the farm family to church on Sunday and livestock or produce to the market the following day). Samson also found success with its trucks, which were built from 1920 to 1923.

Durant's era was over, and so was Samson's, despite their innovations in the market: air-powered wrenches for faster assembly-line work; a franchise dealer system, which required each dealer to be competent to service and repair tractors; selling on time; and what was probably the first water-bath air filter in the industry.

Durant was imaginative, a gifted promoter, and a great salesman, but not sound in planning. Tractor production at the Samson plant lasted until late in September 1921, although 1922 models were made, and then the Samson era ended.

Sawyer-Massey

When it came to tractors, Sawyer and Massey did things backwards, They held on to the principles of steam engines long after it was obvious to just about everyone

Long before the Republican Contract With America, Samson (and before that the Janesville Machine Company) released their own contracts with farmers, "the first progressive sales agreement ever entered into by any manufacturer." This contract was set for the dealers. Samson advertising, however, made little difference, and the company folded for good in the 1920s. The Samson plant was converted into a GMC auto and truck-assembly plant.

else that the new world for farming was gasoline and kerosene tractors. In fact, Sawyer and Massey separated because of the debate over which to build, steam, or gasoline/kerosene tractors.

In 1835, John Fisher moved from New York State to the pioneer town of Hamilton, Ontario, on the edge of Lake Ontario. He began with a small shop that was destined to become one of the largest threshing machinery industries in Canada. His shop was small and he had few tools, but he was an enterprising man and the following year, 1836, he constructed the first threshing machine ever built in Canada. Although it was crude, it worked well and excited a great deal of interest among the settlers who only had the flail to laboriously beat the heads out of their grain.

Suddenly, Fisher saw the possibilities; but he didn't have money to go deeply into making threshing machinery. His cousin, Dr. Calvin McQuesten of Lockport, New York, did, and the two entered into a partner-

ship called Fisher and McQuesten. A few years later three Sawyer brothers, nephews of Dr. McQuesten, came to work for the company. They took on more and more responsibility as the original founders grew older.

After the death of John Fisher in 1856, the name was changed to L. D. Sawyer and Company. The factory, known as the Hamilton Agricultural Works, turned out reapers, mowers, and other implements in addition to separators, horsepower, and tread mills.

As years went by, the company made portable steam engines, horse-drawn machinery, and became Canadian agents for Aveling and Porter road rollers, which were made in England.

According to Merrill Denison in *Harvest Triumphant: The Story of Massey-Harris,* "Another

Left
Sawyer-Massey made separators and threshers, and eventually had a monumental effect on the Massey-Harris company. The two companies worked closely while distributing their different threshers throughout Canada, and Massey-Harris eventually developed their full-line concept because of their association with Sawyer-Massey.

In Canada, this about 1913 Sawyer-Massey was called a 68 horse, which put out about 22 horsepower. Very few of these early machines are found in running condition. Minnesota farmer Daniel Roen of Comstock has two of them, and intends to build one running model out of them.

development of this period which was to have a marked influence in Massey-Harris policy at a later date was the purchase by H.A., C.D., and W.E.H. Massey of a 40 percent interest in the L.D. Sawyer Company of Hamilton, one of the largest makers of steam tractors and threshing machinery in the Dominion. The company was then reorganized as the Sawyer-Massey Company Limited. While no corporate relation was ever developed between the concern and Massey-Harris, the two worked closely in the distribution of threshing machinery in Canada and the association was to have a curious influence on the larger firm at a later stage of mechanization." Thus began the full-line principle.

Early traction engines and portables were all of the return flue type; but in the late 1880s, a change was made to the open bottom, locomotive type boiler without a dome. Hundreds of little 13-horsepower simple, single cylinder, side-mounted engines were built in the 1890s. Soon Sawyer and Massey was turning out 18-, 20-, and 22-horsepower engines for the eastern trade.

This Sawyer-Massey steam traction engine was a side-cranker with a return flue boiler, and it burned coal, wood, or straw. The men, Sawyer and Massey, split up because of their differences on whether they would continue to make steam machines, or go into the seeming wave of the future, gasoline tractors.

Sawyer-Massey made this 22-45 tractor and perhaps because of it, Sawyer and Massey ended up splitting, because the Masseys objected to putting all their energies into making steam traction engines when they figured it was pretty obvious that the future was in gas tractors.

Scientific Farming Machinery Company made this tank-tread 25-50 as part of their line. Called the Mark 4, it sold for nearly $3,800, and resembled other tank-tread vehicles of the time, most notably the Bates Steel Mule. This compact caterpillar would, Scientific claimed, exceed the work of an ordinary six- or eight-plow tractor, although it possessed only three tiller units.

To make sure Western Canada's burgeoning market wasn't overlooked, a large warehouse was built in Regina to supply the prairie needs, and the demand for heavy plowing engines was met by designing a rear-mounted engine which was built in both simple and tandem compound sizes up to 35 horsepower. Except for the rearrangement of the gears and the omission of springs, the engines were practically the same.

A year after its merger with Alanson Harris in 1891, Massey indulged its interest in steam. It bought into the L.D. Sawyer Company, of Hamilton, Ontario, which had been producing portable steam engines since the 1860s. The infusion of Massey money expanded steam traction engine production. At the time Massey joined it, Sawyer was producing single-cylinder locomotive-type steamers. Massey-funded improvements led to the development of double-cylinder engines producing as much as 35 horsepower.

Sawyer-Massey also paid attention to the coming force of the gasoline engine. Curiously enough, they began working with gasoline engines in a backwards way, beginning with the larger 76-horsepower size, with steam engine road wheels and gearing, and then creating succeeding models in smaller sizes, but with the same slow speed motor and same general design. This method has not always been successful, because what large engines need isn't always what smaller engines need, and the ratios don't always work. Steamers as large as 76 horsepower were offered, and gasoline tractors as powerful as 27-50 hp were produced.

Like many of the seminal companies in making tractors and early farm equipment, disagreements arose over the direction the company was taking. The gasoline engine market was the object of the dispute, and led the Masseys to separate from the Sawyers in 1910.

The battle for supremacy between steam and gasoline took place in a series of plowing demonstrations staged first in Winnipeg and then in Fremont, Nebraska. The first of the great trials was staged in 1908 and rivaled the earlier binder trials in the interest they aroused. At the time, Western Canada was the world's most important tractor market, and in the first two contests Sawyer-Massey Canadian steam tractors held their own against the field. By 1910, however, gasoline and kerosene had established their supremacy to all except the diehard advocates of steam.

Despite the fact that the two companies never merged—Sawyer and Massey-Harris—the Sawyer company had an effect on Massey-Harris, showing it that gasoline engines were the wave of the future, and in 1910, Massey-Harris entered the gasoline-engine market.

Curiously enough, even though Sawyer and Massey disengaged in 1910, the Sawyer-Massey name continued to be used (on machinery) into the mid-1920s, when it disappeared forever.

SCIENTIFIC'S PRINCESS PAT

The early 1920s were a time of thinking big, of yelling big, of claiming big, and Scientific Farming Machine Company of Minneapolis was a product of its times, and so it also thought big. In 1917, they offered their new tractor to the U.S. Government with the claim that it would help win the War (World War I; of course, they were not the first tractor company to use this ploy to get itself some attention). It was claimed to be a great invention that would bless humankind.

But to think big and yell big you have to have something worth thinking and yelling about, and as hundreds of tractor companies joined the market about this time, that "something" had to be unique and different.

The Princess Pat "Once-Over" Tractor Tiller was certainly that. At a 1919 show, crowds gathered around this new tractor-tiller because there was nothing else like it in the entire show. The name also was a draw, and it was named the "Once-Over" because it plowed, disked, harrowed, fertilized, seeded, rolled, and packed the ground in one trip over the field, supposedly making a perfect seed bed in one operation. The Princess Pat could replace the efforts of several men, horses, or a large tractor pulling five or six different kinds of farm implements and requiring several weeks of time. For whatever reason, just after World War I the concept of everything rolled together in one was an attractive one (convertible tractor-auto companies and combination trucks-tractors-and-cars companies were springing up all over).

This is how the Princess Pat "Once-Over" Tractor Tiller worked: the plow shares dug into the soil, and pushed the furrow slice backwards, as usual. But instead of the furrow falling to the ground, it instead hit a ver-

The Model 6 Princess Pat "Once-Over" Tractor Tiller had an average drawbar pull of seven to nine horsepower when operated purely as a tractor. It had two forward speeds and one reverse. It used a standard LeRoi four-cylinder, four-cycle, slow-speed heavy-duty engine with a 3 1/8x4 1/2-inch bore and stroke. It also had a self-starting device activated from the driver's seat and dual brakes. It was nine feet four inches long, five feet high, almost five feet wide, and weighed 1,400 pounds.

tical whirling shaft fixed with a series of curved knives, blades, or teeth. The same engine that ran the tractor operated this shaft and when the shaft was propelled at high speed, the teeth engaged the furrow slice as it came off the moldboard and the soil was thoroughly pulverized; in fact, the teeth cut, tore, scratched, bit, and kicked the furrow slice into fine particles; and afterwards all that remained was an aerated field of soil—an ideal and perfect seed bed—smooth, level, and completely tilled from the top to the bottom of the furrow cut. No lumps even as big as a walnut were left, the literature claimed.

To prove its point in the advertising it showed two views of the same field, one using the Princess Pat, the other, conventional horse-drawn equipment. Unfortunately, they used different parts of the fields; a much more convincing test would have been using the clodded-up already-other-tractor-done part of the field to show the difference. Other parts of the machine sowed seed and dropped in fertilizer at the same time.

Director Warsham of the University of Minnesota said, "Every hour a farmer uses the 'Once-Over'

Tiller, he saves 35 minutes of his own time and 1 hour and 45 minutes of horse labor."

Scientific Farming Machinery Company was organized in 1916 by Thomas W. Hicks, and a year later offered the government their machines to help win the war. The government took the offer seriously, having the Princess Pat demonstrated at the government farm in Washington, D.C., at the suggestion of the U.S. Senate committee on agriculture, and with the permission of the United States agricultural department, gained with the assistance of Senator Knute Nelson of Minnesota.

Additionally, Princess Pat operated in front of heads of agricultural departments of all the allied nations under the late Lord Rhondda, formerly food director of the British Empire. It was highly recommended by Mr. Edge, chief controller of the farm machinery department of the ministry of munitions for the British government.

It was sold to a dozen different nations, besides the United States It claimed to increase crop production by 21 percent—five bushels where there used to be four—claimed it would "revolutionize farming," "in all the world, no other tractor like this," "it finishes what other tractors start," and so on.

Several different machines were made, including versions of the Princess Pat, and a Tank-Tread 25-50. Scientific Farming Machinery Company expanded into Canada in 1919.

A couple of companies—perhaps the same one—were opened in New York, the "Once-Over" and U.S. Farming Machinery Company to take care of the trade there, as well as overseas trade.

In 1918, the Vigilance Bureau (which monitored advertising) of Washington, D.C., had some concerns about an advertisement for Scientific, which claimed, "The U. S. Government has declared us a 'war essential' industry and so licensed us—and with a good financial statement, bank references, a strong board, and a going business to back you up, plus being coached and fully equipped with all elements that make for success—you should and must succeed in closing your man."

A letter from the Vigilance Committee said, "We interpret this statement to mean that this stock has been approved by the Capital Issues Committee, and respectfully inquire if this is the case. If not, would there be any other sense in which the expression 'The United States Government has declared us a war essential industry' could be used?" No record exists of a reply or action, although it seems the advertisement was not used after 1918.

"Science" was a big buzzword at the time. Farm magazines of the time talked about how science had aided agriculture. *Farm Implements and Tractor* says in its February 28, 1919, issue, "This is an age of scientific agriculture, and in no industry is progress more noticeable than in that of agriculture. The up-to-date farmer of today owes his success to the application of new and intelligent methods. The improved tilling machine here described will, in the next few years, elevate farming out of the rut of chance and circumstance, into the avenue of scientific certainty. As to whether the machine will live up to the promise of its manufacturers, the Scientific Farming Machinery Company of Minneapolis… is, of course, to be demonstrated."

Scientific's third product was the Mark 4, a horse-drawn "once-over" tiller to be used on small farms. It was demonstrated and sold abroad for two years before it was brought to the United States. The word "scientific" was a buzzword of the day, as science came into play in the lives of farmers. Evidently Scientific wanted to take advantage of that.

Evidently, it wasn't. One of the major reasons was perhaps what made it most unique: the rotating teeth to the right side of the plow. On a windy day (or even a calm one) with dirt exploding in all directions right under one's chin didn't make for an appetizing day of work. Though comfort was not a huge item to past farmers, added discomfort certainly wasn't desired.

The agricultural and national depression struck the United States in the early 1920s, and farm machinery companies died like proverbial flies, including Scientific Farming Machinery Company, which was no longer seen after 1923.

SHEPPARD

The Sheppard diesel tractor just might be the best tractor that never made it. The R.H. Sheppard Company was founded in 1935 by Richard Harper Sheppard when he purchased a one-story building in Hanover, Pennsylvania. The Sheppards were noted for horse races and shoes. The company also manufactured the Kintzing wire cloth loom, floor polishers, and gasoline engine generator-sets for farm use. These products provided the basis for the diesel engine's development. When R.H. graduated from college, his father set him up in the diesel engine business.

The first Sheppard diesels were manufactured experimentally in 1933. Twenty different models were developed and marketed throughout the world. These engines were used to power generator-sets, pumps, lifeboat engines, rescue craft, marine power plants, and farm tractors.

During World War II, the Sheppard diesel found a great market in the military. All of these diesels were low-pressure injection systems. This system was very unusual, and the Sheppard was one of the few diesel engines that utilized that type of fuel supply system. It was unique, inexpensive, and serviceable, but because of its unusual characteristics, it was difficult to get the trade people to recognize it.

References differ on when Sheppard entered the tractor manufacturing business; however, work started in 1933, but the first Sheppard tractors—the SD-1, a small

One of Sheppard's advertising directions was the claim that their diesels cut fuel costs by 75 percent. Ironically, even farmers who witnessed the tractor using minute amounts of fuel figured it was just a trick, because it just didn't seem possible.

Right
The earliest entry of Sheppard into the tractor field came in 1948 in the form of a Sheppard diesel engine designed to fit into the Farmall M that allowed the Farmall tractor to enjoy all the fuel savings benefits of the Sheppard. Partly because of the success of these kits, Sheppard began building their own tractors in 1949. Only a few Farmall kits were made before Sheppard decided to build their own tractor.

This Sheppard SD-3, like all the Sheppard SD tractors, had no magneto, carburetor, or spark plugs. One farmer said it shelled corn at the rate of 270 bushels every 16 minutes and in 4 1/2 hours of continuous operation used only six gallons of gasoline. Perhaps the motto of the Sheppard Company might have been, "good work is not always rewarded." Despite the tractors assets, it did not sell well.

single cylinder air-cooled diesel tractor, more a garden tractor than a farm tractor—didn't appear until 1949.

Sheppard's first idea in 1948 was to replace the standard engine in a Farmall M with a Sheppard diesel. Only a few were built.

After the diesel was tested in the Farmall M, from that point it kind of snowballed. Sixty days from the time they decided to build their own tractor, they had the first Sheppard built. Unfortunately, when the tractor steered left, the tractor went right. But there wasn't enough time before a Pennsylvania farm show to fix it, so the first one that went out in January 1949, when steered left, it went right. Perhaps that was one of the reasons the Sheppard tractors failed.

Robert Chase, a former representative for Sheppard Company, says the Sheppards were a wonderful and powerful tractor. "This was fifty years ago, and everybody was very conservative. So it was pretty difficult to get new ideas into the market. Sometimes you could sell a tractor to a farmer who couldn't get a John Deere, Oliver, Case, IH, or any of those others, and I think that's part of what Sheppard was hoping."

Sheppard had a simple system for naming their tractors—SD3 simply stood for "Sheppard Diesel with three cylinders." Their other systems were simple, too, like the fuel injection system, and their method of selling the tractor, which required that all payments for the tractor had to be received at the factory before the tractor was shipped. Even a millionaire who visited Sheppard, trying to get a Sheppard without paying for all of it at one time, came away empty-handed, told he'd get the tractor when the money was all at the factory.

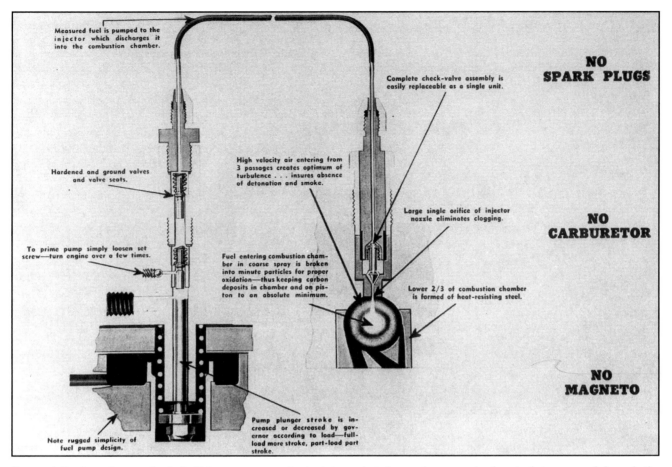

Measured fuel is pumped to the injector which discharges it into the combustion chamber.

Complete check-valve assembly is easily replaceable as a single unit.

NO SPARK PLUGS

Hardened and ground valves and valve seats.

High velocity air entering from 3 passages creates optimum of turbulence . . . insures absence of detonation and smoke.

Large single orifice of injector nozzle eliminates clogging.

NO CARBURETOR

To prime pump simply loosen set screw—turn engine over a few times.

Fuel entering combustion chamber in coarse spray is broken into minute particles for proper oxidation—thus keeping carbon deposits in chamber and on piston to an absolute minimum.

Lower 2/3 of combustion chamber is formed of heat-resisting steel.

NO MAGNETO

Note rugged simplicity of fuel pump design.

Pump plunger stroke is increased or decreased by governor according to load—full-load more stroke, part-load part stroke.

Sheppard diesels used a very simple fuel injector pump, so simple that people today say they can make them in their own workshops. In the day of the Sheppard, demonstrators would use only a screwdriver, crescent wrench, and pliers, to take the fuel injection pump off the engine, take it apart, and then put it back together and put it on the engine again right in the field. Farmers had difficulty believing that process, because most other fuel injection systems could be taken apart only in an atmospheric-controlled room, or else dirt and grit would get inside and cause problems.

But the three-cylinder diesel tractor set up some of its own roadblocks. At that time, anything other than a one-, two-, four-, or six-cylinder wasn't an acceptable design. That Sheppard was a private entrepreneur building his own engine didn't help either.

For his honeymoon, Chase took a trip to Hanover, Pennsylvania, to work in the Sheppard factory for a week, to learn about the Sheppard engine. "My background is as an electrical engineering graduate, so up at the factory I was able to learn a lot of these more intimate things that you wouldn't learn out in the field if you were just a dealer. I got to hear a lot more stuff in the factory than most people would have, I think."

Using that knowledge, Chase says he did a series of impressive demonstrations on farms: First, he took the injector pump off the engine, using just a screwdriver, pair of pliers, and a crescent wrench, and then put it back together right there in the field. No other injector pump could do that. Others needed an atmospheric-

controlled room, otherwise air grit would create problems, but not so with the Sheppards.

Then he would start the machine right up and run it. But he says it seemed like it was a fantasy to a lot of the farmers. In spite of the simplicity, the farmers and people who were interested were really scared of buying them.

"Another test involved a John Deere G, the work-horse farm tractor of the time, and a Sheppard, and putting a gallon of fuel in each. The Sheppard would run three times as far as the G, and those guys would think I had done something they weren't seeing to the Sheppard to get it to do that. It was unbelievable to them, just too good to be true."

Sheppard tractors had a couple of problems, however. First was paying for them. No tractor was delivered until the entire payment for the tractor was received at the factory in Hanover. In fact, Sheppard very politely told a millionaire that they had a policy there, and he didn't care about financial status, everybody stuck to the policy. No one got a tractor until the money was paid in full at the factory. No CODs. That meant farmer or dealer financing, a real handicap, especially since John Deere and IH had just begun floor planning.

One perceived problem involved the oil. They had a very long oil change interval. Some people said they advised changing oil in the spring and the fall or at 1,000 hour intervals. Consequently many came down with crankshaft problems. Also, Sheppard diesels used non-detergent oil.

Chase sees the oil controversy differently. "You never changed the oil in the Sheppard engine," he says. "You changed the filter. It was a dry-sump pressure system. The oil was pumped through a mechanical cleanser first, and then into a fiber-type filter before it went into any part of the engine, onto the bearing surfaces. When the oil got dirty, you changed the master fiber filter, which was about a gallon filter, and your oil would clear up again. Everything was pressure lubricat-

ed. They had an engine running for 10,000 consecutive hours on the same oil: that's five years!" If you used detergent oil, you lost your warranty.

Another problem was starting the tractors. They were direct-start diesel, with a mediocre heating system on the last cylinder. The manifold had a kind of a toaster-wire thing, and then you had a pump on the dash that you could inject raw diesel fuel into this last cylinder. But it just shot a solid stream of fuel instead of a spray like modern diesels. The fuel was above compression pressure, but not much. Then you had a stainless steel power cell where the fuel started burning, and then went out into the cylinder. When it got down to 40 degrees or below it was extremely hard to start unless you pulled them. That seemed to be the biggest complaint about the Sheppard. They also manufactured a number of implements to go along with the tractor.

"What's always amazed me," Chase says, "is the simplicity of the low-pressure injection system that the Sheppards used. I've got a little machine shop, and I can

The Sheppard SD-2 easily handled a pair of 14- or 16-inch plows ("Walks away with them," the company claimed), and could handle three of each in many cases. The SD-2 was touted as the ideal tractor for a farm that needed a tractor to do a wide variety of important work. One testimonial from a Pennsylvania farmer said he cut 15 acres of hay with an SD-2 and only used 34 cents worth of fuel.

make almost any part for a Sheppard except the casting of the engine itself. I can make the injector nozzle, the injector bodies, the pumps, almost anything."

Chase says "There are engineering problems with the Sheppard tractor that could easily be corrected—you've got to remember that if you go back fifty years, metallurgy was very different, and it has changed tremendously during these fifty years. They've learned a lot about pouring castings and restricted areas and things like that, which were some problems in the Sheppard cylinder head. I still feel like it was and is a product that could be competitive today, if it was put back on the market."

But as an orphan tractor, it never will be back on the market.

SILVER KING

One day in 1934 after the Fate-Root-Heath Company of Plymouth, Ohio, had sold rights to its Plymouth name for a measly dollar to Chrysler Company, the principals of the company were sitting around a conference table trying to figure out a new name for their Plymouth tractor.

They wanted "King" because they felt they had the king of tractors, but all the good combinations with king seemed to be taken. One of the board members had brought a bouquet of silver foliage from a plant at home, and their eyes lit upon its color. Someone came up with the idea, "Let's call it Silver King." And that's the way it came about.

The real history began in 1884 when John Fate founded the J. D. Fate Company, in Plymouth, Ohio, for the purpose of manufacturing extrusion machines used in manufacturing brick and drain tile.

Four years later, J.D. Fate Company merged with the Freeze Company of Galion, Ohio, and became Fate-Freeze, then Fate-Gunsaullus Company, then J.D. Fate. In 1895 the Root Brothers Company, which manufactured cobbler's supplies, became associated with Heath Foundry.

In 1909, the concept of a Plymouth car was developed in a machine shop of the Plymouth Motor Truck Company in Toledo. In 1910, they came out with a Plymouth car, powered by a four-cylinder engine and a dou-

The Silver King in this photo is a Model R38.

ble-disc truck transmission with a chain drive to the axle. The Plymouth became a trade name of the company long before Chrysler thought of it. That same year the production plant was moved to Plymouth. During this same year, J.D. Fate Company built its first locomotive.

In 1919, the J.D. Fate Company, the Root Brothers Company, and the Heath Foundry all joined to form the Fate-Root-Heath Company. The three men involved were J. D. Fate, Percy Root, and Charley Heath.

Until 1933, Fate-Root-Heath concentrated on locomotives and clay industry machinery. But on November 10, 1933, they unveiled their first Plymouth tractor. That was the Plymouth 10-20, powered by a 20-horsepower four-cylinder motor with a 3x4-inch bore and stroke. The transmission was a four-speed, and the "transport" fourth gear provided a startling 25 miles per hour top speed.

The Plymouth tractor combined the hood and gas tank into one unit. Emblazoned prominently on the vee'd radiator shell was the name "Plymouth." They built 232 Plymouth tractors, when suddenly Chrysler Corporation came knocking. Chrysler had come out with their Plymouth car in 1928. But Fate had built the Plymouth car in 1910, long before Chrysler, so they had the rights to the name. Everything becomes sketchy about here, but what is clear is that Chrysler sued them.

Chrysler felt the Fate-Root-Heath Company was infringing upon their right to use the name Plymouth. When the Fate-Root-Heath Company produced records to show its predecessor company had used the Plymouth name many years before, Chrysler and the Fate-Root-Heath Company came to an agreement. Fate-Root-Heath opted to sell the name to Chrysler for one dollar rather than wrangle with a larger and richer company and perhaps court bad press. So that meant the Plymouth tractor had to be renamed, as mentioned, to Silver King.

The Silver Kings were the same basic design as the Plymouth tractors. Only a couple of things were changed. In the Plymouths, the hood and the gas tank were all one

piece. The Plymouth had a four-piece radiator that sat right out front and wasn't protected. In the Silver Kings they made a two-piece gas tank and a different grill.

According to the *Silver King News*, the Silver King tractor became such a solid tractor because their development of industrial locomotives gave them some advantage and ideas of what is needed on the farm. In its infancy, Silver King created a sensation—not only in appearance but in performance. This was a new and different kind of tractor.

The Fate-Root-Heath Company had excellent concept people. Silver Kings were the first tractors to come out with a starter, lights, and rubber tires. Silver Kings were said to be built nearly as perfect as possible. Employees of the Fate-Root-Heath Company pledged themselves to quality first.

By 1936, the Silver King offered an unusual three-wheel tractor powered by the same Hercules engine. Another three-wheeler, the Model 600 (and subsequent 660 and 720 models), appeared in 1940, powered by Continental engines. Road gear on these tractors hit a top speed of 30 miles per hour. Later models returned to four-wheel configurations.

Most Silver Kings were sold to farmers for hauling, cultivating, and general use, or were purchased by the state highway department, which bought a surprising number of them to mow strips of grass along Ohio roadsides. Silver King was one of the first tractors to prove that rubber tires could hold up in a farm work environment.

Legend has it that Mae West, queen of the Silver Screen, kept a fleet of Silver Kings, buying 90 to tend her vineyard in California. She wanted them to keep making them, so the story goes.

Silver Kings were made in colors besides silver. The Ohio highway department had yellow ones, some counties had them painted orange. Some of those yellow ones are pretty rare.

Only 8,600 Silver Kings were made from 1934 to 1954. Successful tractor companies of the era made more tractors in one year—or even in a good month—than Fate-Root-Heath made in its history. The company's best year was 1937. They made 1,000 that year, because the mower industry was good.

Fate-Root-Heath also made an industrial model tractor. People say all the tractors that Fate-Root-Heath made were almost custom-made. Because they made a lot of different models—ten models in one particular year—all of them are a little bit different from each other.

So what turned the tide against the Silver Kings?

The main factor was that Charley Heath, the man who ran the tractor division in the late 1940s, wanted to get out of making tractors. No one else would take over. So the company sold all their rights to Mountain States Fabricating Company in Clarksburg, West

Left
Silver King tractors were originally named Plymouth tractors. When the mighty Chrysler Corporation sued the relatively small Fate-Root-Heath (the company that built Silver Kings), the name went to the deeper-pocketed company. Fate-Root-Heath probably had the legal right to the name, as they had been using it since 1909, but Chrysler had more legal might. Fate-Root-Heath accepted a small payment for the name, which was preferable to spending millions to defend themselves in court. This ad depicts the earliest Silver King in 1936. Early Sliver King model names were based on tread width, with the first two digits representing the tread width in inches. The 600, for example, had a 60-inch tread width, the 660 a 66-inch tread width, and so on.

Virginia. About 75 West Virginia Silver Kings were made before that company folded.

Although the tractor story ends here, Fate-Root-Heath made more than tractors. The company made cars, as mentioned above, and also built a few hundred trucks and touring buses. The company turned to locomotives just after the turn of the century, and still makes them in Plymouth today. The company is no longer known as Fate-Root-Heath. They were sold to Harold Schott in 1966, and became a division of Banner Industries of Cleveland, Ohio, in 1969.

The Fate-Root-Heath name was eventually replaced with the name Plymouth Locomotive Works (PLW). Today, PLW has become an employee-owned and -operated company, Plymouth Locomotive International, Inc.

STANDARD

What makes Standard Engine Company of Minneapolis an unusual orphan tractor company is not only that it made small tractors—mostly garden tractors—but also because it existed for such a long time before going out of business.

Standard Engine was incorporated in Minneapolis in 1917, and was still operating in 1951. The Minnesota Secretary of State's office could only say that it was no longer presently in business, as indicated by their "expired" designation, but they didn't know when it had disappeared.

The Standard Engine Company appears to have been a large company, with offices in Minneapolis, New York, and Philadelphia. In a letter from the company sales manager, the Standard tractors are defined: "As the name implies, Standard Tractors are complete power propelled machines, with all the essential parts of big farm tractors, but of a size adapted to the close rows and restricted spaces of truck gardens, home acreages, and general crop small-farms. They plow, disc, seed, cultivate, mow hay or lawns, run belt machinery, in fact handle all the major small-farm tasks; and handle them with far less drudgery than hand methods or far less expense and inconvenience than a horse."

To prove their point, Standard ran ads with pictures of letters they'd received from satisfied customers. In one series of ads, Standard concentrated on the longevity of the tractors: "I am very proud and satisfied with my new Monarch. Before I bought this one, I had owned one of the first Monarch Models put out. It is nearly 30 years old now and still runs, but it is just too tired for hard work. This summer I bought my second standard twin tractor and I am very well satisfied with it. I bought my first one in 1935 and did all the work with it, except fall plowing, on 15 acres of truck garden. I also plowed smaller patches during the summer months."

Other models included the Walsh and the Standard Twin Convertible, a combination riding and walking tractor for small farms.

The sales manager's candor in his letter to a prospective customer was refreshing: "In this discussion of Standard Tractors I have tried to be candid and fair, but perhaps I am biased—I have something to sell." He enclosed some of the letters from satisfied customers to help make his point; those customers ranged from owners of chicken farms, greenhouses, nurseries and florists, even a railroad agent.

Standard also had an installment payment plan, it appears without interest: "Just take your choice of either the 12 monthly or 20 monthly Installment Plans. Start with a small initial investment, and let the tractor pay its own way."

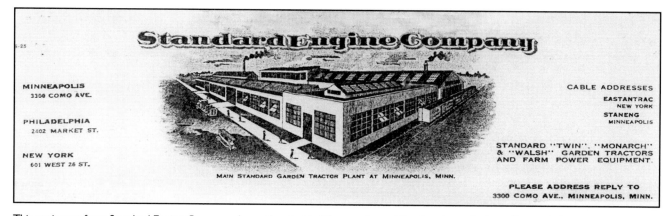

This stationery from Standard Engine Company shows the plant in Minneapolis, and lists locations of other offices and the products the company made. Perhaps more than any other orphan tractor company, Standard used testimonials from people to help sell their machines. One series of ads is totally filled with good news from farmers who used the Standard series of machines.

STANDARD TWIN Convertible

A Quick Change Riding or
Walking Tractor for
Gardens and Small Farms

2 Cylinders
5 H.P. Engine
2 Speeds & Reverse
Power Turn Brakes
and
Pivot Wheeled
Riding Carriage

The Standard Twin Convertible was operated either by driving it from the seat or while walking alongside. The five-horsepower engine was a two-cylinder, the transmission had two speeds forward and one reverse, and the tractor was equipped with a ten-inch plow. Other Standard equipment, like the Walsh, the Monarch, and the Twin, all tillers, changed very little from the 1920s until the 1950s, with the exception of rubber tires being added.

Standard also answered questions about its tractors in ads by using letters from customers, like "Does it handle easy? Is it sturdy? Does it overheat? Does it have enough power: We have a number of different garden tractors around here, but only two that will do a decent job of plowing—one is my Monarch and the other is a Standard Twin owned by my neighbor."

Though the last dated letter was in 1951, there's no proof that was Standard's last year; but it did go under, perhaps that same year, perhaps a number of years later, probably to increasing competition for the garden tractor market, and in the process orphaned its Standard tractors. (Standard Engine Company is not to be confused with Standard Tractor Company, which operated in a number of Minnesota cities—St. Paul, Willmar, Stillwater, Minneapolis—in the 1910s.)

STAUDE MAK-A-TRACTOR

Just make yourself a tractor was the concept of the Staude Mak-a-Tractor Company of St. Paul, Minnesota. "With a Staude Mak-a-Tractor you can plow in the morning," the advertising literature said, "you can do your heavy hauling in the afternoon, and you can drive for pleasure in the evening."

All you needed was a Ford runabout or touring car; you didn't even have to detach the body, bore any holes, take out the rear spring, or take off the running board. "The change can be made from automobile to tractor or from tractor to automobile in 20 minutes." The cost of the add-on equipment ran from $200 to 300.

Bizarre as this sounds, the concept of the multiuse machine was heavily touted in the 1910s. Advertisements would make these claims, it would be assumed,

Staude Mak-a-Tractor company had a high number of strong beliefs. They believed that farmers—and farmers' wives—would be comfortable spending at least 40 minutes a day putting the Staude Mak-a-Tractor parts on and taking them off, the family car. This says nothing about the problems of dirt or wear and tear on a vehicle that wasn't really made to be pulling heavy loads in the field. They also believed that farmers would pay to buy their add-on materials.

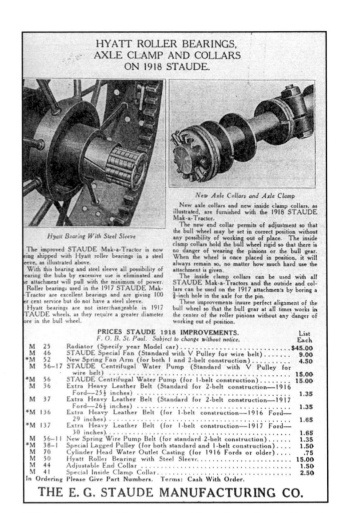

This advertisement hints at the problems that existed with early versions of the Staude Mak-a-Tractor, listing the improvements that had been made from the previous year. Such an ad surely left lingering doubt in any farmer's mind. What else could be wrong with it? What hasn't been fixed?

because the tractor companies were paying for them. But reputable magazines and newspapers also made these claims.

Glenn G. Hayes, editor of *Better Farming*, wrote in a July 1917 editorial to 300,000 farmers, "I have seen this attachment do good work in wheat stubble—replacing four big horses or mules and capable of going day and night if need be. On the road the hauling speed is about five miles per hour. Those same horses would require twenty acres of feed to keep them a year. The farmer who owns a small car and does not investigate the efficiency of this new attachment is blind to opportunity. One has all to gain and nothing to lose in asking his dealer to a show-down on this proposition. I don't know how one can get a 'four-horse team' any cheaper."

Also, the St. Paul *Dispatch* wrote, "St. Paul To Be World Center For Tractors" in a 1917 headline. The account went on to state that Staude was planning to build 50,000 tractors in 1918.

Why Staude intended to build 50,000 tractors is a bit of a mystery. Staude had sold 50 in 1916, and the highest claim (which is disputed) for 1917 was 7,000 units. Staude hoped to sell 50,000 in 1918, and for that reason had increased its capitalization from $150,000 to $5,000,000.

The Staude Tractor was the result of four years' experimenting by Mr. Staude and his staff of engineers. The attachment dropped the final drive ratio way down, so the high-speed power of the auto engine was transferred into the low-speed output necessary for pulling power.

The company claimed that the tractor could be attached to an automobile in 20 minutes. American farmers at that time owned more than 2,000,000 automobiles, each of which could be converted quickly through the addition of the pair of tractor wheels, re-

This Staude Mak-a-Tractor is pulling a pair of plows in northern North Dakota about 1920. The Mak-a-Tractor, along with the other car-to-tractor conversion kits, had limited success.

ducing gears and axles, into serviceable farm tractors. In addition to domestic production, 500 Mak-a-Tractors were shipped to England in 1917.

Though the rhetoric was high, there had evidently been problems with the Mak-a-Tractor, since advertisements are headed "The New 1918 Cooling Equipment." The information says that a series of this cooling equipment was now furnished complete as standard equipment. It made overheating of the Ford engine practically impossible. This extra equipment was furnished with the attachment without additional charge.

Also, the literature says, "Through the use of the improved centrifugal pump, the water in the radiator is moved at the rate of 14 gallons per minute, and does not stay in the cylinder head long enough to raise the water to the boiling point, even under heavy work in hot weather, and yet permits the motor to run hot enough to operate at its best."

Right
Perhaps the simplicity of this advertisement was meant to symbolize the simplicity of putting on and taking off the parts necessary to make a Staude Mak-a-Tractor. Despite the fact that these "tractors" were significantly cheaper than purchasing a separate tractor, the conversion kits were only on the market for a few years.

THE NEW 1918
IMPROVEMENTS OF THE

STAUDE
Mak-a-Tractor
(Trademark Mak-a Reg U. S. Pat Office and Principal Foreign Countries)

MAKE IT
A BETTER TRACTOR

MAKE YOUR
FORD A BETTER CAR

Other advertising literature says there is no unusual strain or pull on the Ford, but that it is actually pushed ahead of the Mak-a-Tractor. All of these point out some problems that were being addressed.

Some of the customer letters tell how the Staude Mak-a-Tractor was used to pull half-ton sucker rods out of oil wells 550 feet deep, as well as for 26 farm uses.

However, like the other combination machines sold to farmers, the Mak-a-Tractor did not make it; it did not make St. Paul the tractor center of the world, nor produce an additional 5 million bushels of grain.

Instead, before 1920, it sank into oblivion, and another tractor dropped down the tubes.

TOWNSEND

The Townsend Manufacturing Company of Janesville, Wisconsin, was famous for an odd reason: they were one of the last to produce a gas engine tractor that looked like a steam engine.

Roy C. Townsend, designer of the Townsend Tractor, was a man who came out of the past. For years he worked for Fairbanks-Morse, and helped develop the Fairbanks-Morse tractors. When they decided to abandon tractors, Townsend broke off on his own. He established himself in Janesville, Wisconsin, in 1915, manufacturing the Bower City Tractor; later the tractors they made were called Townsends. All but one Townsend tractor looked like a steam engine. Their last tractor was the exception.

Perhaps one of the things that weakened the Townsend company was the manufacture of too many different varieties of tractors, which had proved fateful to other tractor companies, especially during the tough economic times, when they would naturally, because of more models, have more money tied up in inventory.

Letters to Townsend Mfg. Company in 1922 were good ones: "With respect to the tractor I bought from you last summer, I am glad to say that it is delivering the goods far beyond my expectations. With this 10-20 tractor I have plowed 300 acres, tandem disked and drilled to wheat 150 acres, tandem disked and drilled to oats 20 acres, and am now breaking prairie sod, pulling a four-disk plow and harrow. The motor works perfectly

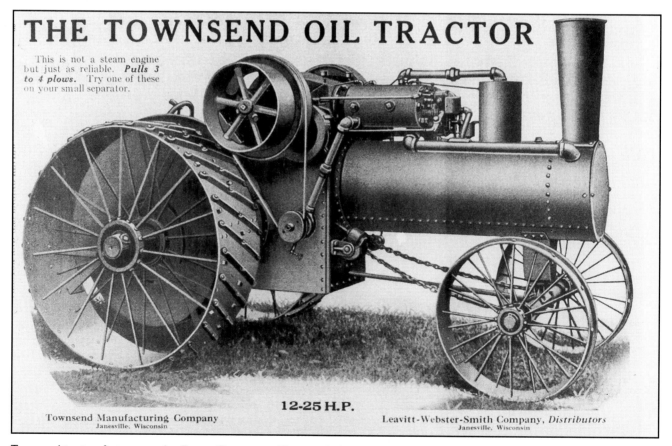

Townsend tractors first appeared as Bower City tractors. Townsend oil tractors, like this 12-25, closely resembled steam tractors. This was no coincidence, as the founder of the Janesville, Wisconsin, company had worked for a steam tractor company.

in this climate. Uses cheap fuel perfectly. …My grief has been little and my running expense very light."

Another letter praised the tractor, and added, "One very important feature of the tractor is the easy access to the working parts, fuel line, clutch, valves, connecting rods, etc. Parts that sometimes need attention, and they can be readily gotten at, will not be neglected. …I consider the tractor good in the drawbar, and when it comes to belt work, it has all of them beat."

An early advertisement proclaimed the Townsend was made just as strong as it looked. It additionally stated it was pleasing to the eye—it certainly was different—and that it is of the most thoroughly tried out construction on the market. The same foundation which is the backbone of any machine, having been used in steam tractors since their origin and no one has ever heard of the boiler under a steam tractor giving out, due to the rack and strain a tractor frame is subjected to. A great many breakages and

undue wear is due directly to the various parts getting out of alignment, due to weak frames.

They also said no fan was needed for the Townsend. They claimed a draft through the radiator was an improvement, as no power was wasted and the draft was increased as the load increased. This was one reason the Townsend was remarkably successful on low grade fuels.

Another ad claims the Townsend is not a steam engine, but just as reliable. But the Depression put the bite on Townsend, just as it did on all the other tractor companies, and in February, 1931, Townsend tractors were to be made henceforth by the La Crosse Boiler Company of La Crosse, Wisconsin, where repairs could also be obtained for old tractors. Three sizes of tractors would be produced, a 12-25 for field work, and a 40-horsepower, and a 60-horsepower size for heavy duty stationary work. R. C. Townsend of the Janesville, Wisconsin, company, was said to be joining the new organization.

The Townsend 30-60 in this photo belongs to Norm Pross of Luverne, North Dakota. It was the largest Townsend built, and still carries the telltale look of the old steam engines, which Townsend wanted to play upon. The 30-60 was a two-cylinder with a 9 1/2x12-inch bore and stroke that ran at 450 rpm. The tractor weighed 12,000 pounds, was 13 feet 8 inches long and 7 feet 2 inches wide.

This advertisement says the Townsend touts the tractor's ability to burn distillate. The company succumbed to the Depression and was sold to LaCrosse Boiler Company of LaCrosse, Wisconsin. The sale was the end of Townsend, as the tractors did not reappear.

Townsend Oil Tractors

are simple and reliable. A size for any farm is available at a price that is right.

Townsend 2-plow 20 H. P. has the least number of parts and will operate on comparatively less fuel and lubricating oil than any tractor made today.

A post card will bring you the whole story. Don't put it off.

Townsend heavy-duty threshing and road engines. Four sizes, 20 to 60 H. P. in the belt.

If you are thinking of buying a tractor for any purpose, you cannot afford to overlook our line, which is the most complete of tractors being made at this time.

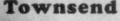

TOWNSEND TRACTOR CO.   Janesville, Wisconsin

This 1925 advertisement for Townsend oil tractors touted the simplicity of the Townsend tractors. A two-plow 20-horsepower tractor is shown at top left. One of the downfalls of Townsend was that they had too many models, and when tough economic times came, as they always seem to in the agriculture field, they had too much inventory and couldn't generate enough cash flow.

Unfortunately, it wasn't long until Townsend tractors were just a memory.

WATERLOO BOY

In a way, it was a rifle cartridge that invented tractors, according to this story. John Froelich of Froelich, Iowa, ran a grain elevator, and sought to make extra money in 1888 by custom combining—running threshing crews in Iowa and South Dakota.

Unfortunately, his J. I. Case steam engine was heavy and clumsy to move and just as likely to set the grain on fire as to thresh.

So he resolved to build a better engine. He and his helper, William Mann, spent hours making their own machine. When they were finished, they put every-

thing unneeded away, fueled it, and cranked it by hand. Unfortunately, it refused to run.

So Froelich took a rifle cartridge, removed the bullet, and stuck the cartridge into the priming cup. There he smacked it with a hammer. Bam! The flywheel spun and the engine started working. Both in forwards and backwards gears. The tractor—or at least a form of it (several others claimed they invented the first tractor) had been invented! He used it successfully during that 1892 year, threshing more than 72,000 bushels.

Froelich was enthusiastic about the possibility of making more of the machines, and selling them. So he and others started Waterloo Gasoline Traction Engine Company in 1893, the first company organized for the sole purpose of developing a tractor (called traction engines at the time). Froelich used a Van Duzen engine and modified it, garnering several patents in the process. Four of the machines were built and two were

This about 1918 Waterloo Boy Model N is grinding feed on a North Dakota farm. This tractor was the first tractor ever tested in the Nebraska Tractor Tests from March 31 to April 8, 1920. About 8,000 Waterloo Boys were sold from 1917 through 1924. The Model N and Model R were very similar and early ones were painted red. The P.J. Downes Company of Minneapolis was the major distributor for Waterloo Boys (among other tractors) in the Upper Midwest. *State Historical Society of North Dakota*

sold, but both must have proved ineffective in the fields, for they were quickly returned. In a sense that was appropriate because that was exactly what happened with many tractor companies who turned out their equipment half-tested.

The disappointment of the return of those early machines was so great that the people managing Waterloo Gasoline Traction Engine Company decided they would continue making stationary gasoline engines to keep the company afloat while it tested and retested the tractors until they could be built properly.

But Froelich wasn't interested in waiting. He wanted to build tractors. So he bowed out. Without him, a new company was formed, called Waterloo Gasoline Engine Company, specializing in the manufacture of stationary gasoline engines. In the meantime, Froelich went off to do his own thing without being held back by rigid ideas of a company he did not own.

The gasoline engines were a mainstay of the Waterloo Gasoline Engine Company. In 1896 they produced another gasoline tractor, but only sold one. An-

other new tractor was designed a year later, with the exact same results.

Also about this time, Louis B. Witry joined the company. He designed the Waterloo Gasoline Engine, which was far superior to anything that had been put on the market at that time, many people said. Demand for the stationary engines was so great that a new plant had to be built.

At the same time, Witry designed a two-cylinder automobile; six of them were sold, but stationary engines were selling so fast that all energies and shop space had to be turned towards making and selling them. The demand for that engine was responsible for the great success of the company as men worked steadily to fill orders from all parts of America and many foreign countries. The company never did come back to making automobiles.

True to their word, tractors had not been forgotten, however. In the early 1910s, the first successful Waterloo tractors were produced, and 20 of the L-A models were sold.

The first Waterloo Boy, the Model R, was brought out in 1914, and 118 were sold in 1914. After soliciting and getting farmer input, and using it to change the design—an enlightened way of doing business—four years later more than 8,000 were sold, and Waterloo Boy tractors were big names and hot stuff. The Model N Waterloo Boy was introduced, and it, too, was a smashing success. The company, which had employed 20 people in 1895, rose to employ more than 1,000. A Waterloo Boy tractor was the first one tested in the Nebraska Tests, in 1920.

World War I ended, and opposition to tractors as farm machinery was ending too, partly because of the lack of horses (average life of horses during World War I was less than two weeks), plus soldier-farmers had seen the advantages of machines. So Waterloo Boys were hot.

So hot that John Deere had been keeping an eye on Waterloo Gasoline Engine Company's success. Mr. Silloway of John Deere wrote at the time, "I believe that, quality and price considered, it is the best commercial tractor on the market today," says John Deere's Company. "The only real competitor it has is the IHC ....The Waterloo tractor is of a type which the average farmer can buy.... We should have a satisfactory tractor at a popular price, and not a high-priced tractor built for the few. Here we have an opportunity to, overnight, step into practically first place in the tractor business.... I believe that we would be acting wisely if we purchased this plant."

At first Deere and Company hemmed and hawed, not positive that that was what they wanted to do. But an ultimatum came down from Waterloo Gasoline Engine Company saying the decision must be made by March 14, 1918.

The 12-24 Waterloo Boy was advertised in 1915 for $750 with the claim that it could plow eight acres a day at 16 cents an acre. It originally appeared on the scene in 1914. In 1915, Waterloo Gasoline Engine Company ran a "Great National Race" contest to see which dealer could sell the most Waterloo Boys. The top 60 were rewarded various Waterloo Boy engines. The company said they had their factory working overtime to produce enough 12-24s to meet demand.

The Waterloo Model R shown in this ad in 1918 has a 25-horsepower engine and could pull three plows. Waterloo Boy built a variety of models between 1914 and 1918, including Models A through M (skipping J). Models A, B, C, and D all had the same engine, a horizontal twin of 24 horsepower. Models E, F, and G used a horizontal twin of 25 horsepower.

The decision by Deere was unanimous to buy the company, which they did for $2,350,000 on March 18, 1918. Waterloo Boy tractors were produced by John Deere and called Waterloo Boys for the next five years, after which Waterloo Boy, and its company, joined the ranks of other orphan tractors, a kinder fate than a lot of orphan tractors, considering that John Deere is one of only a handful of tractor companies still operating today.

Waterloo Gasoline Engine Company is not to be confused with the Waterloo Manufacturing Company of Waterloo, Ontario, an entirely different company which manufactured steam traction engines and tractors until 1925.

Right
This full-page ad for Waterloo Gasoline Engine Company was typical of many advertisements of the day, chock-full of words and information that farmers could sit down and read at a time when life was more leisurely and print advertising was essentially the only way to get the advertiser's message across. This ad ran in 1916. Waterloo Boy was bought out by John Deere in 1918. They retained the Waterloo Boy badge for about five years, before slipping away as orphans.

Orphan Tractor Listing

About 400 tractors were orphaned. Some of these were the actual names of companies; others were tractors made by companies with different names. In several instances, one tractor name covers several tractors made by several different companies, like Montana or Universal.

Abenaque
Acme
Adams-Farnham
Advance
Ajax
Akron
Allen
Allied
Allis-Chalmers
Allwork
American Kerosene
Andrews
Andrews-Kinkade
Angleworm
Antigo
Appleton
Armington
Atlas
Aulson
Aultman-Taylor
Austin
Auto
Automotive
Auto-Tractor
Auto-Track
Avery
Baby Savidge
Bailor
Baker
Bates All Steel
Bates Steel Mule
Bean
Beaver

Bell
Belle City
Beltrail
Besser
Best
Bethlehem
Big Four
Birrell
Blue
Blumberg
Boenker
Boring
Boyer
Boyett
Breed
Brillion
Brockway
Bryan
Buckeye
Buffalo-Pitts
Bull
Bulldog
Bullock
Burn-Oil
Cameco
Cameron
Canadian
Canadian-American
Capital
Centaur
Central
Challenger

Champion
Charter
Chase
Cletrac
Cleveland
Cockshutt
COD
Colby
Coleman
Columbus
Comet
Common Sense
Co-op
Corbitt
Craig
Creeping Grip
Creeping Tiger
Cultor
Custom
Dakota
Dart
Denning
Depue
Derr
Detroit
Diamond
Diamond M
Dill
Dissinger
Dixieland
Eagle
Earthmaster
Eastman

Ebert
EFT
Elgin
Emerson-Brantinham
Essex
Evans
EZ Built
Fageol
Fairbanks-Morse
Farmer Boy
Farmers Oil
Farmer's Tractor
Farmer Tractor-Truck
Farm Horse
Farmaster
Farquhar
Fitch
Flour City
Ford
Fox
Franklin-Flexible
Frick
Friday
Gaar-Scott
Galloway
Gamer
Gasport
Gearless
Gehl
Geiser
General
Gibson

Gile
Gilson
GO
Golden West
Goodfield
Graham-Bradley
Grain Belt
Gramont
Gray
Great Western
Hackney
Hagan
Happy Farmer
Harris
Hart-Parr
Heer
Heider
Heinze
Hession
Hicks
Hill
Hockett
Hollis
Holmes
Holt
Holton
Hoosier
Huber
Hume
Hunter
Ideal
Illinois
Indiana
Imperial
Ingeco
Iron Horse
Joliet
Joy-McVicker
JT
Jumbo
Kardell
Kay-Gee (KG)
Kaywood
KC
Kenison
Keystone
Kimble & Dentler
Kingwood
Kinkhead
Kinnard
Klumb
Knapp
Knudsen
LaCrosse
Lambert
Lang
Laughlin
Lauson
Lawter
Leader
Leonard
Lenox
Liberty
Lightfoot
Line Drive

Linn
Lion
Little Bear
Little Chief
Little Giant
Little Oak
Little Traction Gear
Lombard
London
Long
Love
MacDonald
Magnet
Marshall
Massey-Harris
Master Huffman
Maxim
Maytag
McKinney
Mead-Morrison
Me-Go
Michigan
Middletown
Midget
Midland
Midwest
Minneapolis
Minneapolis Moline
Minnesota
Minnesota Giant
Mohawk
Moline Universal
Monarch
Montana
Moon
Morris
Morton
Motox
MPM
Multipedal
Multi-Tractor
National
Nelson
Nevada
New Age
New Britain
New Elgin
New Giant
Nichols-Shepard
Nilson
Ohio
Oil-Pull
Olds
Oldsmar
Oliver
Olmstead
One Man
Once-Over
Otto
Pacemaker
Pan
Paramount
Parker
Parrett
Peoria

Petro-Haul
Phoenix
Pioneer
Planet
Plow Boy
Plow Man
Pontiac
Porter
Port Huron
Post
Powell
Power
Prairie Dog
Prairie Queen
Princess Pat
Providence
Plymouth
Pullford
Quincy
Ranger
Rigid-Rail
R & P
Reed
Reeves
Rein Drive
Reliable
Rex
Rock Island
Rogers
Royal
Royer
Rumely
Russell
Saint Paul
Samson
Sandusky
Savage
Sawyer-Massey
Sexton
Sharpe
Shaw
Shawnee
Shelby
Sheppard
Shirk
Short-Turn
Sidehill
Silver King
Simplex
Square Turn
Standard
Standard-Detroit
Star
Staude
Stearns
Steel Hoof
Steel King
Sterling
Stinson
Stockton
Stover
Strait
Strite
Stroud
Sun

Superior
Sweeney
SWH
Sylvester
Tank-Tread
Terratrac
Thieman
Tioga
Thomson
Thorobred
Topp-Stewart
Toro
Townsend
Traction
Transit
Traylor
Trenam
Triple-Tractor
Triumph
Trojan
Trundaar
Turner
Twin City
Uncle Sam
Union Bulldog
Union Sure-Grip
United
Universal
Universal Farm Motor
US
Utility
Van Nostrand
Vaughn
Velie
Victor
Victory
Vincennes
Vim
Wadsworth
Waite
Wallis
Ward
Waterloo Boy
Waterous
Weber
Webfoot
Wellington
Western
Wetmore
Wharton
Wheat
Whitney
Wichita
Wilson
Winnebago
Wisconsin
Wizard
Wolverine
Yankee
Yankee Boy
York
Ypsilanti
Yuba
Zellea

Index